How to Make the Most of this Phrasebook（この本の使い方）

 **❶ Say, "Sumimasen." to someone nearby.**

 **❷ Let the person you're talking to see that the book has Japanese translations.**

For starters, smile and say, "Sumimasen" (Excuse me). Starting off a conversation in Japanese is the best way to get help from strangers.（まずは笑顔で「すみません」の一言から質問してみましょう）

Many Japanese think their poor "Japanese English" is a source of misunderstanding and embarrassment. If they shy away from you, assure them this phrasebook has Japanese translations.（この本には日本語の訳もついているので、英会話が苦手でも大丈夫です）

 **❸ Point to the word as you say it.**

 **❹ Ask a Japanese person to say the word and then repeat it.**

If you're worried about your pronunciation, you can show the phrasebook to the person you're talking to and make sure your message is getting across. For basic rules on Japanese pronunciation, turn to page 4.（発音に自信がなくても、指さしながら使えます。4ページの「発音のガイド」も参考に）

There is nothing like imitation when you're trying to learn a new language. If you think you're mispronouncing a word, ask the person you're talking to to correct you. That way, you can turn your daily encounters into fun-filled, on-the-spot language lessons.

When you learn by watching and listening to native s repeating after them, you'll be amazed at how fast you ma vocabulary words, turn to P.103 to see our 2000-plus wo くできなかったら、話しかけた日本人に教えて 日本人の方も英会話練習にぜひご活用ください）

The Original "POINT-AND-SPEAK" Phrasebook
（旅の指さし会話帳　日本）

㉑

JAPAN

written by Toshiya Enomoto
榎本年弥・著

Table of Contents（目次）

Section 1（第１部）
The Original "POINT-AND-SPEAK" Word Sheet Pages
（『旅の指さし会話帳』本編） 7

Section 2（第２部）
Tips on understanding Japanese people
（日本人を理解するためのヒント） 85

Section 3（第３部）
Glossary (English - Japanese)
（英語→日本語　単語集） 103

Section 4（第４部）
Glossary of Japanese Holidays, Nations of the World, etc.
（日本の祝日、世界の国名など） 121

Acknowledgements & Author's Notes
（あとがき／協力者へのお礼） 126

Theme（ページのテーマ）

空港
At the Airport
Arriving in Japan, changing to domestic flights, etc. 8

Highlights（ページで話せる内容の例）

Page number（ページ番号）

Transportation 移動
空
At the Airport
Arriving in Japan, changing to domestic flights, etc. 8

Geography 地理
日本の地
Geography of Japa
Names and locations of Japanese prefectures 18

Life in Japan 生活
礼儀と習
Manners & Custom
Previewing unique Japanese manners & customs 28

Shopping 数字・買い物
お金と数
Money & Number
Japanese currency, counting in Japanese 36

Japanese Culture 文化
一年と天
Japanese Calenda
Weather, climate and seasonal events in Japan 46

Enjoying Meals 1 食事1
有名な日本
Well-known Japanese Fo
Ordering sukiyaki, sushi, tempura & Japanese noodles 54

Enjoying Meals 2 食事2
野菜と果
Vegetables & Fruit
Vegetables, fruits, seasonings, and cooking utensils 62

When & What Time? 約束
時間と時
What Time?
Asking the time, making appointments 7

Emergencies トラブル
薬局・病
Drugstores & Clinic
Buying medicine, parts of the body 74

Other その他
家族・人間関係・恋
Family & Romanc
Discussing family and romantic relationships 8

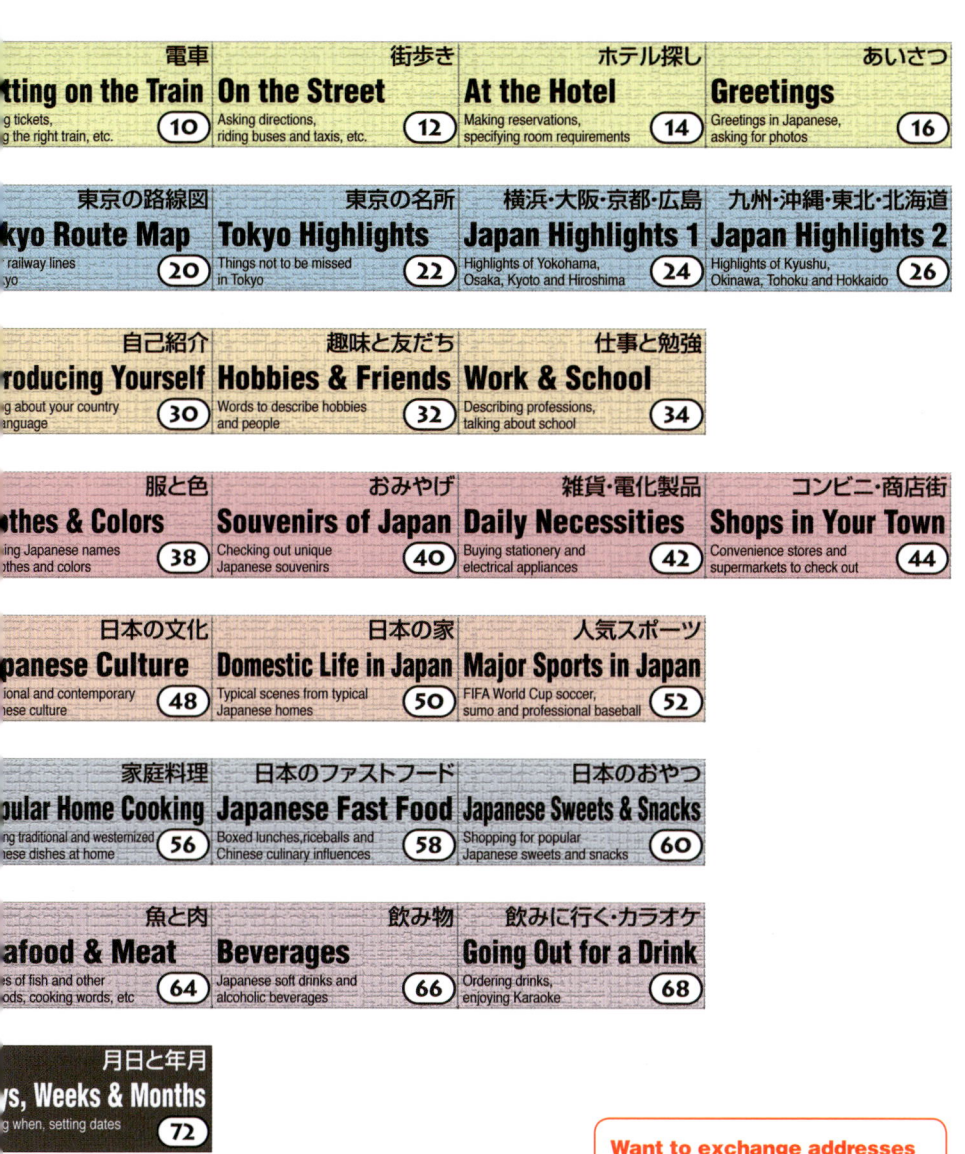

Basic Rules on "Romanized" Japanese Pronunciation

Basic Vowels (基本となる母音　あ・い・う・え・お)

[a]　"a" as in "hat" in British English（イギリス英語のhatのaに近い音）
　　or "o" as in "hot" in American English（またはアメリカ英語のhotのoに近い音）
[i]　"i" as in "sit", but sounds more like "i" than "e"（sitのiに近い音）
[u]　"oo" as in "look"（lookのooの部分に近い音）
[e]　"e" as in "bed"（bedのeに近い音）
[o]　"o" as in "lock" in British English（イギリス英語のlockのoに近い音）

Prolonged Vowels (長音：母音を伸ばす音)

[aa]　"ar" as in "market" in British English（without exaggerating "r" sound）
　　　イギリス英語のmarketの中のarの部分に近い音（Rは強調しない）
[ii]　"ee" as in "feel"（eastのeaないしはfeelのeeに近い音）
[uu]　"oo" as in "boot"（bootのooの部分に近い音）
[ee]　Prolonged "e" sound of Japanese, which has no English equivalent.
　　　（日本語の「え」の音を伸ばしたもので、英語には同等の発音はない）

* Note that [ei] is pronounced more like [ee], and [ou] is pronounced more like [oo] in actual conversation. So we use [ee] instead of [ei], and [oo] instead of [ou] for this phrasebook.
　　　（会話では、「エイ」と表記される音が「エー」、「オウ」と表記される音が「オー」と発音されるため、本書では実際の発音を優先して表記しています）

[oo]　"aw" as in "saw" in British English　（イギリス英語のsawの中のawに近い音）

* Note that in public places you will see alternate spellings like "ā," "ī," "ū," "ē," "ō," but they are pronounced in the same way.
　　　（公共の場所での標識などでは、同様の音を表わすのに、"ā," "ī," "ū," "ē," "ō," といった表記がされています）

Confusing Double Vowels (注意したい二重母音)

[a'u]　(sounds similar to "ou" as in "out")　　[a'i]　(pronounced "a" "i" and not [ei]])
[i'e]　(sounds similar to "ye" as in "yes")　　[u'e]　(sounds similar to "we" as in "wet")
[e'a]　(pronounced "e" "a" and not [i:])　　　 [o'e]　(pronounced "o" "e" and not [ou])

* When "Romanized," some double vowels (diphthongs) are quite confusing for English speakers. To avoid confusion, a comma is inserted between vowels to show that they are read the Japanese way.
　　　二重母音の表記には、英単語のスペリングと似たものもありますが、読み方は異なります。例えば、auはautomaticなどの英単語では「オー」ですが、日本語のローマ字表記では「アウ」となります。

Tricky Consonants (注意したい子音)

[f]　as in [fu] sounds more like "hu"　　　[r]　sounds more like [l] than [r]

* Japanese "Romanization" uses the letter [r] rather than the letter [l], but [r] in Japanese "Romanization" is pronounced more like [l]. The position of the tongue is halfway between the English [l] and [r] sounds.
　　　日本語のローマ字表記では、ラ行音の表記にLではなくRを代用していますが、音の印象はどちらかと言えばLに近い音に聞こえがちです。また、日本語の「fu／ふ」は、英語と違って下唇を噛まずに発音します。

（ローマ字表記された日本語の基本の発音ルール）

Double Consonants （促音—つまる音について）

Watch out for the following double consonants.
[kk]   as in "chekku (check)"
[pp]   as in "kippu (ticket)"
[ss]   as in "shusshin (where you are from)"
[tt]   as in "natto (fermented soybeans)"
When pronouncing these double consonants, try inserting a slight pause before the consonant.

　[kk]、[pp]、[ss]、[tt]といった促音（つまる音）の表記に注意。このように表記される音は、促音の前に少し間を入れて発音します。

Hyphenation （読み仮名のハイフン化）

Normally this is not part of standard "Romanization." However, some "Romanized" words are much easier to read for English speakers when hyphenated. Long words, as well as hard-to-read words from foreign languages, are hyphenated as necessary.

　通常、日本語をローマ字表記する際には、ハイフンは使用しません。が、英語を話す人たちにとっての読みやすさを考え、長い言葉などには必要に応じてハイフンを入れて表記しています。

Romanization （ローマ字表記について）

A new, easier-to-read "Romanization" system is needed to better represent the actual sounds of Japanese in this international day and age. Japan, however, has yet to discard the old system of "Romamization." No matter how confusing it is for English speakers, that is what you see in public places, magazines, language classes, etc. A completely new phonetic system could put you at a disadvantage. Therefore, changes are kept to a minimum. Learn the actual Japanese sounds as you use this phrasebook to talk to the Japanese people you meet.

　日本語の音をわかりやすく表記するには、現在のローマ字表記に代わるシステムが必要です。しかし、公共の場所や雑誌、会話のレッスンなどで、皆さんが目にするのは昔ながらのローマ字表記です。本書では、旅先や日本語のレッスンで読者の皆さんが困らないように、なるべくローマ字表記をベースとして、発音を表記しています。正しい日本語の発音は、この本を手がかりとして知り合った、日本の人たちから学んでゆきましょう。

(to be continued on P.102/ P 102に続きます)

And Finally...Translation （最後に英訳について）

Quite a few Japanese words and phrases defy translation. For example, when a newcomer first meets his "host," it is polite to say "osewa ni narimasu (I appreciate your looking after me.)" Phrases like this do not exist in English language. In Japanese, words mean more than just what they appear to say. They often represent the concepts that are important in Japan. At times, English cannot adequately convey these concepts. But in editing this phrasebook, every attempt was made to describe words and concepts which have no equivalents in English language.

　本書では英語にしにくい日本語も、わかりやすく説明するようにしています。しかし、日本語には英訳できない言葉がかなりあります。「お世話になります」のような日常的なセリフも、文化的な違いを考えたら直訳では意味が通じません。日本語を理解するには、表面的な言葉の意味よりも、日本的な概念や文化的背景が大切な場合が多いからです。こうした場合英語は、コミュニケーションのための道具として割り切って考える必要があります。

Special features of this phrasebook（この本のしくみ）

39 practical examples of daily conversation you're likely to encounter

（実用的な会話のシーンを39場面収録）
This phrasebook features 39 highly practical situations with useful everyday phrases. These pages help you learn the "Point-And-Speak" method.

Colorfully illustrated pages

（カタコト会話に威力発揮！ カラフルなイラスト）
Colorful illustrations make the book fun and easy to use. If you can't pronounce the word you want, just point to the picture!

Situational indexes for greater ease of use.

（場面別インデックスで使いやすさアップ）
On every page you'll find a situational index. The index comes with handy references for all the conversational situations covered in the book.

Cross-referenced for convenience

（関連した内容が探しやすい）
Important words are marked with arrows that direct you to related words and phrases in other sections of the book.

Easy-to-read pronunciation guides

（読みやすさを意識した発音のガイド）
Our pronunciation guides are a departure from conventional "Romanization" of Japanese sounds. We use a slightly different system to make pronunciation easier for English speakers. Read the tips on P.4-5 to learn the basics of Japanese pronunciation. If you're not sure, just ask your new Japanese friend!

Glossary with over 2,000 entries and pronunciation guide

（発音ガイドつき——2000語収録の単語集）
Use the glossary to find just the word you're looking for. More than an appendix, glossary entries were specifically chosen to compliment the situational conversation pages by the "on-the-street" linguist author himself.

The back cover of the book is your portable "chalkboard".

With a water-soluble marker you can make your point in writing. Just wipe it clean after use. （水性ペンなら裏表紙に何度もメモ書きできます）

Designed for travelers on the move, this phrasebook uses high-quality paper that is sturdy, yet flexible enough to fit easily in your hand or pocket. （折り曲げて持ち歩きやすいように、本書は特別な紙を使っています）

Section 1
第1部

The Original "POINT-AND-SPEAK" Word Sheets

『旅の指さし会話帳』本編　指さしシート
Pain-free Guide To Spoken Japanese

At the Airport 空港 *kuukoo*

Excuse me.
すみません
sumimasen

Thank you.
ありがとう
arigatoo

Where?
どこですか？
doko des-ka

immigration
入国審査
nyuukoku shinsa

yes
はい
hai

no
いいえ / いえ
iie/ie

sightseeing
観光
kankoo
→ P.18~27

business trip
出張
shucchoo

→ P.34

Working Holiday
ワーキングホリデー
waakingu horidee

studying in Japan
日本に留学
nihon ni ryuugaku
→ P.35

stay
滞在
taizai
→ P.72 → P.124

about
大体
daitai

1 week
1週間
isshuu-kan

2 weeks
2週間
ni-shuu-kan

passport
パスポート
pasupooto

return ticket
帰りの航空券
ka'eri no kookuu-ken

1 month
1か月
ikka getsu

1 year
1年
ichi-nen

Interpreter, please. *
通訳をお願いします
tsuuyaku o onegai shimas

I live in Japan. → P.18
日本に住んでます
nihon ni sunde-mas

More slowly, please. **
ゆっくりお願いします
yukkuri onegai shimas

I have just come back from my country
里帰りしてました
sato-ga'eri shite-mashita → P.122

* There are always English-speaking immigration officials around. If you don't see any, maybe you can help me sell them my phrasebook. (英語のできる係員が必ずいるものだけど、カタコトの人ばかりだったら、一応この本をすすめとくように）

Transportation 移動

At the Airport

Where? どこですか？ *doko des-ka*	**baggage** 荷物 *nimotsu* 	**claim tag** 引き換え証 *hikika'e-shoo*
customs 税関 *zeekan* 	**currency exchange** 両替所 *ryooga'e-jo* → P.36 	**restroom** トイレ *toire* 
things to declare 申告する物 *shinkoku suru mono*	**Yes, I have.** あります *arimas*	**No, I haven't.** ありません *arimasen*
leaving the country 出国 *shukkoku*	**international flight** 国際線 *kokusai-sen* 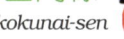	**departure lobby** 出発ロビー *shuppatsu robii*
transfer 乗り継ぎ *nori-tsugi* 	**domestic flight** 国内線 *kokunai-sen* → P.18	**check-in counter** 出発カウンター *shuppatsu kauntaa*
carry-on baggage inspection 手荷物検査 *te-nimotsu kensa*	**no smoking** 禁煙 *kin'en*	**smoking area** 喫煙所 *kitsu'en-jo*
boarding gate 搭乗ゲート *toojoo geeto*	**This is my flight.** (Show your ticket.) この便です *kono bin des* 	**plane ticket** 航空券 *kookuu-ken* 
→ P.74 **drugstore** 薬局 *yakkyoku*	**shop(s)** 売店 *baiten*	→ P.18-27 **tourist information** 観光案内所 *kankoo an'nai-jo*

* * Japanese people will enjoy helping you with your speaking. They have suffered through English in school so they know what it's like. (外国人のたどたどしい日本語で平気？ 英語に苦労してきた日本人だ、わかってくれるさ)

Getting on the Train 電車 *densha*

Excuse me. すみません *sumimasen*	**Thank you.** ありがとう *arigatoo*
Where? どこですか？ *doko des-ka*	**Please write it down.** 書いて（下さい） *kaite (kudasai)*

Foreign Tourist Information Center 外国人観光案内所 *gaikoku-jin kankoo an'nai-jo* → P.18~27	**New Tokyo (Narita) International Airport** 成田空港 *narita-kuukoo* 

 | **Where?**
どこですか？
doko des-ka? | **Which railway line?**
何線（ですか）？
nani-sen (des-ka) → P.20

hotel → P.14 ホテル *hoteru*	**station** 駅 *eki*	**location** 場所 *basho* → P.12	**name** 名前 *nama'e*

How much? いくらですか？ *ikura des-ka* → P.36	**ticket** 切符 *kippu*	**place to buy** 売り場 *uriba*	**telephone** 電話 *den'wa*

Keisei Skyliner * (for Nippori and Ueno Sta.) 京成スカイライナー *keesee sukai-rainaa* 	**Narita Express** (for Tokyo, Shinjuku, Ikebukuro Sta.) 成田エクスプレス *narita ekusu-puresu* 

to ~ ～まで *made*	**To Tokyo** 東京まで *tookyoo made*	**Limousine Bus** → P.20~24 (for various parts of central Tokyo) リムジンバス *rimujin basu*

⑩ * If you are not in a rush, take a local Keisei train and enjoy watching the local species in the "Japanese human zoo." （時間に余裕があれば京成の普通列車で、日本人という生き物を観察してみよう。"人間動物園" ジャパンにようこそ！）

Transportation 移動

Getting on the Train

Which train goes to Tokyo? 東京行きはどれ（ですか）？ *tookyoo-iki wa dore (des-ka)* → P.20	**Which platform?** 何番線（ですか）？ *nam'ban-sen (des-ka)*
How many stops from here? ここからいくつ目（ですか）？ *koko kara ikutsu-me (des-ka)*	**How long does it take?** 時間はどの位（ですか）？ *jikan wa dono-kurai (des-ka)* → P.70
Do I have to change trains? 乗り換えは？ *norika'e wa* → P.20	**Which station?** どの駅（ですか）？ *dono eki (des-ka)*	**Please write it down.** 書いて下さい *kaite kudasai*

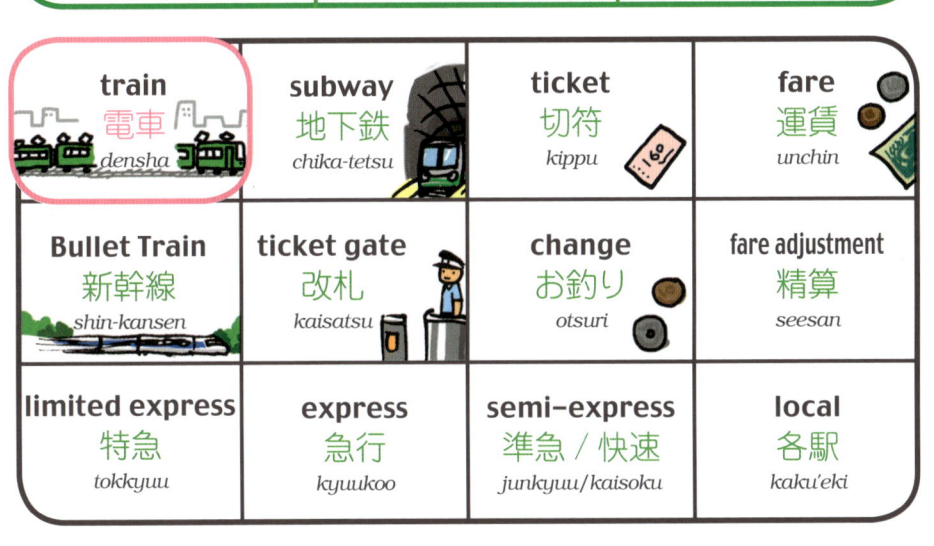

train 電車 *densha*	**subway** 地下鉄 *chika-tetsu*	**ticket** 切符 *kippu*	**fare** 運賃 *unchin*
Bullet Train 新幹線 *shin-kansen*	**ticket gate** 改札 *kaisatsu*	**change** お釣り *otsuri*	**fare adjustment** 精算 *seesan*
limited express 特急 *tokkyuu*	**express** 急行 *kyuukoo*	**semi-express** 準急 / 快速 *junkyuu/kaisoku*	**local** 各駅 *kaku'eki*

shop/news stand 売店 *baiten*	**newspaper** 新聞 *shimbun*	**chewing gum** ガム *gamu*	*** * "Ekiben" boxed lunch** **(bought at station)** 駅弁 *eki-ben*
vending machine 自販機 *jihanki*	**crowded** 混雑 *konzatsu*	**rush hour** ラッシュ *rasshu*	**restroom** トイレ *toire*

* * Some Japanese (myself included) enjoy "ekiben" box lunches and beer on the Bullet Train, only to fall into a blissful sleep, punctuated by occasional snores! (新幹線で駅弁とビールをやると、幸せそうにいびきをかいて眠ってしまう日本人もいる。私もそうだ…)

On the Street 街歩き *machi-aruki*

Where (is ~)? どこですか？ doko (des-ka)	**How long/How far?** どの位 dono-kurai	**time** 時間 jikan	**distance** 距離 kyori
Please write it down. 書いて下さい kaite (kudasai)	**(on the) map** 地図 (に) chizu (ni)	**address** 住所 juusho	**name** 名前 nama'e
convenience store コンビニ kombini → P.44	**bank** 銀行 ginkoo → P.37	**post office** 郵便局 yuubin-kyoku → P.74	**coin-operated laundry** コインランドリー koin randorii → P.44
supermarket スーパー suupaa	**Internet cafe** ネットカフェ netto kafe	**drugstore** 薬局 yakkyoku	**police box** 交番 kooban → P.78
coffee shop 喫茶店 kissa-ten	**foreign book store** 洋書店 yoosho-ten	**hospital/clinic** 病院 byoo'in → P.76	**restroom** トイレ toire
department store デパート depaato P.38~43	**restaurant** レストラン resutoran → P.54~59	**Japanese-style bar & grill** 居酒屋 izaka-ya → P.68	**shopping mall** 商店街 shooten-gai → P.44
Where should I go for ~ ? どこがおすすめ (ですか)？ doko ga osusume (des-ka)		**eating out** → P.54~59 食事 shokuji	**fun/entertainment** 遊び asobi
shopping 買い物 kaimono → P.40	**souvenirs** おみやげ omiyage	**groceries** → P.62 食料品 shokuryoo-hin	**clothes** → P.38 洋服 yoofuku

*Taking a taxi in Japan can be interesting. Drivers don't usually speak foreign languages, but they don't expect tips either and give out free "pocket tissues". (日本のタクシーはチップを取らず、逆にティッシュをくれたりします)

Transportation 移動

On the Street

nearby 近い *chikai* 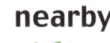	**You can walk.** 歩ける *arukeru* 	**this way** こっち *kocchi*	**that way** あっち *acchi*	**over there** 向こう *mukoo*
straight ahead 真っ直ぐ *massugu* 	**cross** 渡る *wataru* 	**road, street** 道 *michi* 	**intersection** 交差点 *koosaten* 	
turn 曲がる *magaru*	**corner** 角 *kado* 	**traffic light** 信号 *shingoo*	**pedestrian crossing** 横断歩道 *oodan-hodoo* 	
left/right 左／右 *hidari/migi*	**first/second** 1つめ / 2つめ *hitotsu-me/futatsu-me*	**third/fourth** 3つめ / 4つめ *mittsu-me/yottsu-me*	**Which one?** どれ（ですか）？ *dore (des-ka)*	

far 遠い *tooi* 	**You can't walk.** 歩けない *aruke-nai*	**How long/How far?** どの位（ですか）？ *dono-kurai (des-ka)*

taxi * タクシー *takushii*	**To Tokyo Station.** 東京駅まで *tookyoo-eki made*	**How much?** いくら（ですか）？ *ikura (des-ka)*

bus **  バス *basu*	**destination** 行き先 *ikisaki*	**(Please) tell me when we get there.** 着いたら教えて（下さい） *tsuitara oshi'ete (kudasai)*

place to ride 乗り場 *noriba*	**multiple tickets** 回数券 *kaisuu-ken* 	**fare finder ticket (for a bus)** 整理券 *seeri-ken*	**farecard** 運賃カード *unchin kaado*

** Front-boarding buses generally charge a flat fare that you pay when you board. Rear-boarding buses usually issue numbered fare-finder tickets. (通常、前乗りのバスは乗車時に定額を、後乗りのバスは整理券に応じた運賃を後払いする)

At the Hotel
ホテル探し
hoteru-sagashi

Do you know any good hotels?
良いホテル、ない（ですか）？
ii hoteru nai (des-ka)

Japanese-style hotel
旅館
ryokan

Japanese-style bed & breakfast
民宿
minshuku

room rate
料金
ryookin

location
場所
basho

reservation
予約
yoyaku

telephone number
電話番号
den'wa bangoo

ホテル探し

Do you (they) have ~ ?
〜ありますか？
arimas-ka

air-conditioner
エアコン
e'akon

Internet access
ネットアクセス
netto akusesu

restaurant
レストラン
resutoran

refrigerator
冷蔵庫
reezooko

room service
ルームサービス
ruumu saabisu

fax service
ファクス
fakkusu

bathroom
バス・トイレ
basu/toire

bed
ベッド
beddo

futon
布団
futon

bathrobe
浴衣
yukata

What time? → P.70
何時？
nan-ji

check-in
チェックイン
chekku in

check-out
チェックアウト
chekku a'uto

breakfast
朝食
chooshoku

(Please) book the room for me.
予約、お願い（します）
yoyaku onegai (shimas)

date
日にち
hinichi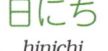

→ P.37
number of guests
人数
ninzuu

→ P.72

room
部屋
heya

single
シングル
shinguru

double
ダブル
daburu

twin
ツイン
tsuin

Western-style room
洋室
yoo-shitsu

Japanese-style room
和室
wa-shitsu

smoking
喫煙
kitsu'en

* **no smoking**
禁煙
kin'en

14 * Japanese people have been imitating American culture for more than 50 years, but somehow they have been slow to adopt a U.S.-style non-smoker's movement. （アメリカの真似が多い日本だけど、嫌煙家への配慮を真似するのは遅すぎた印象だ）

Transportation 移動

At the Hotel

I have a reservation. 予約しました yoyaku shimashita	**The name is ~ .** ~です ~des	
I don't have a reservation. 予約してません yoyaku shite-masen	**Do you have any vacancies?** 空いてますか？ aite-mas-ka	

Phrases				
~ , please. お願いします onegai shimas	**front desk** フロント furonto	**manager** 支配人 shihai-nin	**wake-up call** → P.70 モーニングコール mooningu kooru	
(Please) tell/show me. 教えて（下さい） oshi'ete (kudasai)	**telephone** → P.82 電話 den'wa	**outside call** 外線 gai-sen	**room-to-room call** 内線 nai-sen	**Internet** インターネット intaanetto
(Please) fix ~ . 直して（下さい） na'oshite (kudasai)	**shower** シャワー shawaa	**bath** 風呂 furo	**toilet** ** トイレ toire	**air-conditioner** エアコン e'akon
(Please) change ~ . 替えて（下さい） ka'ete (kudasai)	**lights** 電気 denki	**television** テレビ terebi	**alarm clock** 目覚まし mezamashi	**room key** 鍵 kagi
(Please) give me ~ . ~下さい ~ kudasai	**pillow** 枕 makura	**bathrobe** 浴衣 yukata	**sheets** シーツ shiitsu	**room** 部屋 heya
	soap 石鹸 sekken	**towel** タオル ta'oru	**map** 地図 chizu	**ashtray** 灰皿 haizara

** Staying in a budget hotel? Make sure they have a western-style restroom ("yooshiki toire"). Or try a Japanese-style restroom and let me know what you think.（安さ勝負の宿では洋式トイレのチェックを。和式に挑戦？ 感想待ってるぞ）

Greetings あいさつ aisatsu

  **Good morning.** おはよう（ございます） *ohayoo (gozaimas)*	 **Good afternoon.** こんにちは *kon'nichiwa*
  **Good evening.** こんばんは *kombanwa*	 **Good night.** おやすみ（なさい） *oyasumi (nasai)*
* **Hello./Hi.** どうも *doomo* 	* **Thanks.** どうも *doomo*  
 **How are you?** 元気（ですか）？ *genki (des-ka)*	 **How's it going? And you?** どうですか？ *doo des-ka*
Fine, thank you. おかげさまで *okage-samade*  	**Doing great.** 元気（です） *genki (des)* 
Keeping busy. 忙しい（です） *isogashii (des)*  	**So-so.** まあまあ（です） *maamaa (des)* 
Surviving. 何とか（やってます） *nantoka (yattemas)* 	**Things are tough.** 大変（です） *taihen(des)* 

* Another tricky phrase is "Chotto." Depending on the context, it can mean "a little," "No, thanks." or "I don't want to talk about it." "Chotto" tricky, isn't it? (「ちょっと」にも、「少し」、「いりません」、「話したくない」など複数の意味がある。「ちょっと」難しい？)

Transportation 移動

Greetings

Thank you (very much).
ありがとう（ございます）
arigatoo (gozaimas)

** No, thank you.
結構です
kekkoo des

You're welcome.
どういたしまして
doo itashi-mashite

My pleasure.
こちらこそ
kochira-koso

(I'm) sorry.
ごめん（なさい）
gomen (nasai)

No problem.
大丈夫（です）
daijoobu (des)

(Please) be careful.
気をつけて（下さい）
ki o tsukete (kudasai)

Good bye.
さようなら
sayoonara

I must be going.
失礼します
shitsuree shimas

Allow me to leave before you do.
お先に
osakini

Let's meet again.
また会いましょう
mata aimashoo

See you.
じゃあね
jaa-ne

See you later.
またね
mata-ne

Good to see you again.
先日はどうも
sen'jitsu wa doomo

Long time no see.
久しぶり
hisashi-buri

Can I take a photo?
写真、いい（ですか）？
shashin, ii (des-ka)

Sure.
どうぞ
doozo

Please don't.
困ります
komarimas

Please take a photo(of/for me).
写真お願い（します）
shashin onegai (shimas)

** "Kekkoo des" can be tricky, too. Some people use it to mean "That's enough/That's all right." Want more language tips? Kekkoo des-ka? (「結構です」を「それで良しとします」の意味で使う人もいる。もっとアドバイス欲しい？ 結構ですか？)

17

Geography of Japan
日本の地理
nihon no chiri

Where are you from?	Which prefecture?	Which city?
（ご）出身は？	何県（ですか）？	何市（ですか）？
(go) shusshin wa	*nani-ken (des-ka)*	*nani-shi (des-ka)*

日本の地理

East	West	South	North	What is it famous for?
東	西	南	北	何が名物（ですか）？
higashi	*nishi*	*minami*	*kita*	*nani ga meebutsu (des-ka)*

18　＊ "Meebutsu" is the local product or food for which an area is well-known. Sadly, some "meebutsu" become embarrassingly kitschy souvenirs. (名物は地元の誇りだが、時には恥ずかしくなるほどおバカなおみやげに加工されてたりする)

Geography 地理

1. Hokkaido 北海道
2. Aomori 青森
3. Akita 秋田
4. Iwate 岩手
5. Yamagata 山形
6. Miyagi 宮城
7. Fukushima 福島
8. Niigata 新潟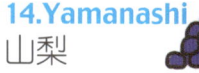
9. Toyama 富山
10. Ishikawa 石川
11. Fukui 福井
12. Gifu 岐阜
13. Nagano 長野
14. Yamanashi 山梨
15. Aichi 愛知
16. Shizuoka 静岡
17. Tokyo 東京
18. Kanagawa 神奈川
19. Chiba 千葉
20. Saitama 埼玉
21. Tochigi 栃木
22. Gunma 群馬
23. Ibaraki 茨城
24. Osaka 大阪
25. Kyoto 京都
26. Nara 奈良
27. Hyogo 兵庫
28. Shiga 滋賀
29. Mie 三重
30. Wakayama 和歌山
31. Hiroshima 広島
32. Okayama 岡山
33. Tottori 鳥取
34. Shimane 島根
35. Yamaguchi 山口
36. Tokushima 徳島
37. Ehime 愛媛
38. Kagawa 香川
39. Kochi 高知
40. Fukuoka 福岡
41. Saga 佐賀
42. Nagasaki 長崎
43. Oita 大分
44. Kumamoto 熊本
45. Miyazaki 宮崎
46. Kagoshima 鹿児島
47. Okinawa 沖縄

Geography of Japan

Depicted alongside prefecture names are their well-known "meebutsu." Talk to the locals to find out more. (県名の隣の絵は各地の名物。地元の人に話しかけて色々聞いてみよう)

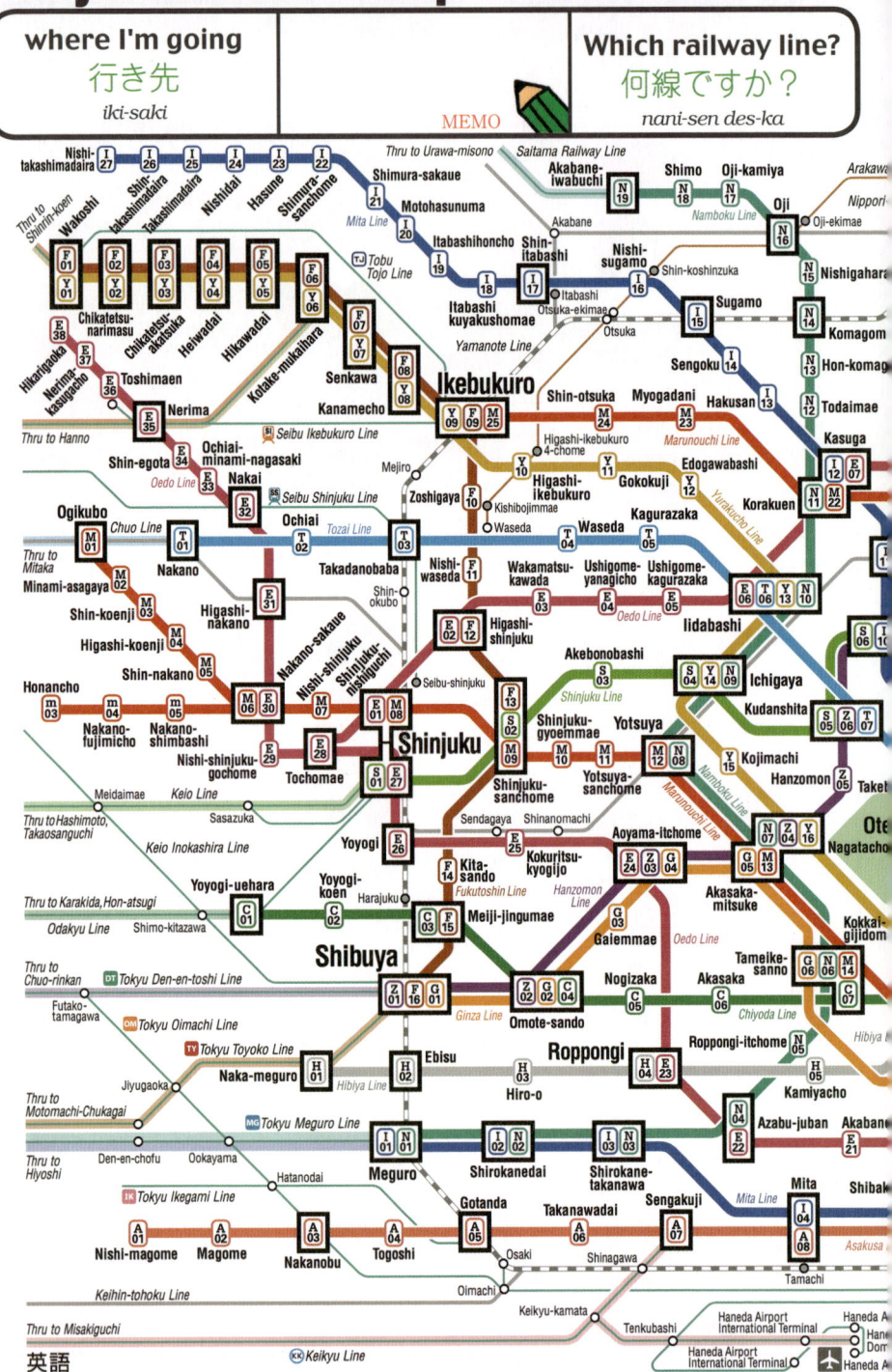

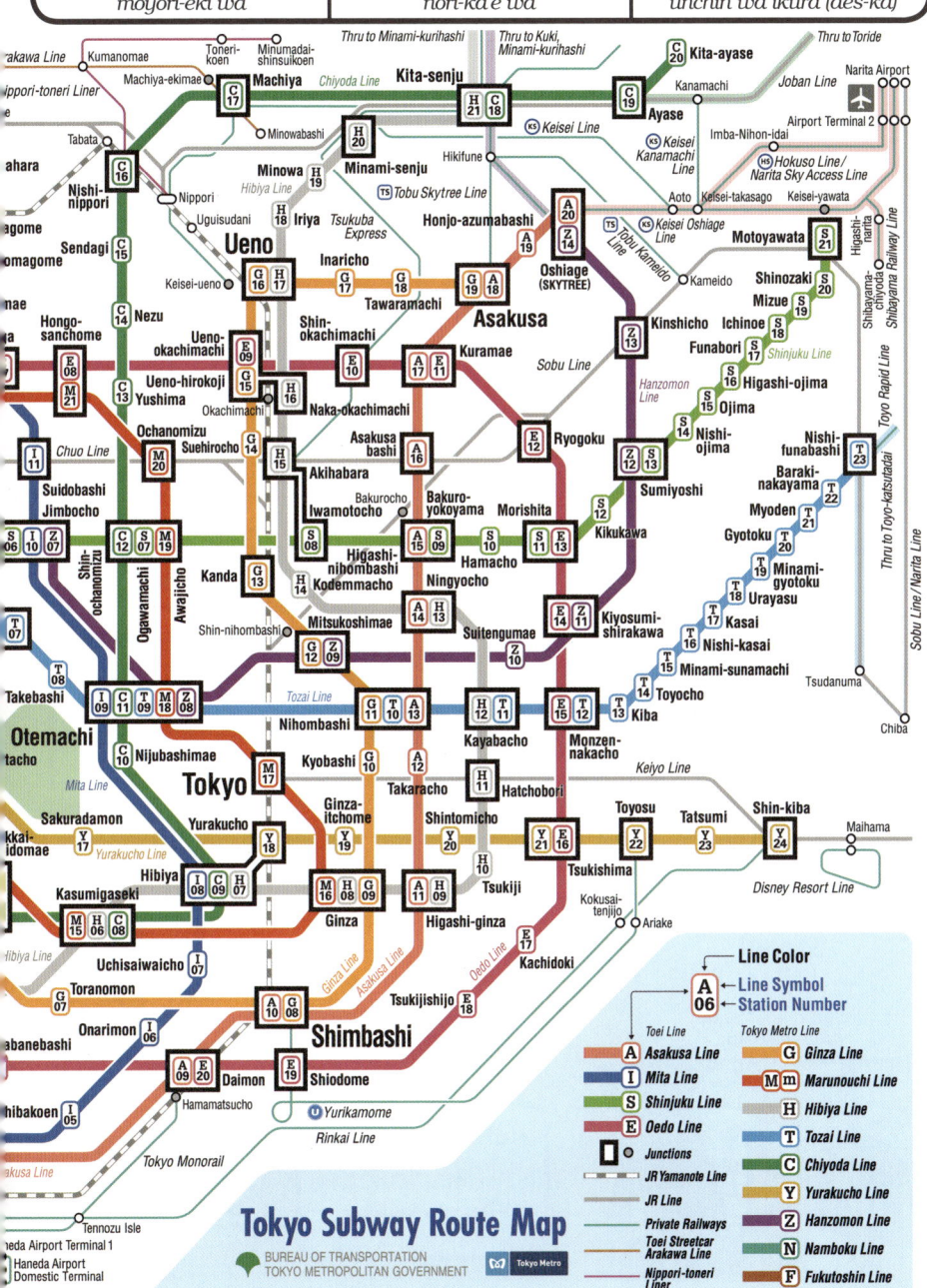

Tokyo Highlights 東京の名所 *Tokyo no meesho*

Which railway line? 何線（ですか）？ *nani-sen (des-ka)*	Which station? 何駅（ですか）？ *nani-eki (des-ka)*
*How many minutes from the station? 駅から何分（ですか）？ *eki kara nam-pun (des-ka)*	Which exit? どの出口（ですか）？ *dono deguchi (des-ka)*

東京の名所

Animate main store
アニメイト本店
animeito honten
(Ikebukuro Sta.)

SUNSHINE 60　JR. Yamanote Line
IKEBUKURO

Tokyo Dome City
東京ドームシティ
tookyoo doomu sitii
（Suidobashi Sta.）

Takeshita-dori Street
竹下通り
takeshita-doori
(Harajuku Sta.)

SHINJUKU

HARAJUKU

SHIBUYA

Imperial Palace
皇居
kookyo
(Tokyo Sta.)

Shibuya "Center" Street
渋谷センター街
shibuya sentaa-gai
(Shibuya Sta.)

Tokyo Tower
東京タワー
tookyoo tawaa
(Onarimon Sta.)

Haneda Airport
羽田空港
haneda kuukoo
(Haneda-Kuko Sta.)

HAMAMATSUCHO

22　* Most Tokyo highlights are within walking distance from a train station. Give your legs a workout and go home fitter!!（東京の見所のほとんどは最寄駅から歩ける。しっかり歩いて、健康になって国に帰ろう！）

Geography 地理

(Please)tell/show me. 教えて（下さい） *oshi'ete (kudasai)*	** highlight/attraction 見所 *midokoro*	famous local food/souvenir 名物 *meebutsu*

Tokyo Highlights

Asakusa Nakamise shopping arcade
浅草仲見世
asakusa nakamise (Asakusa Sta.)

Tokyo Skytree
東京スカイツリー
tookyoo sukai tsurii (Oshiage/Skytree Sta.)

Ueno(-Koen) Park
上野公園
u'eno kooen (Ueno Sta.)

Ame-yoko Shopping Street
アメ横
ame-yoko (Ueno Sta.)

Kokugi-kan Sumo Arena
国技館
kokugi-kan (Ryogoku Sta.)

Akihabara (town of electronics & otaku culture)
秋葉原
akihabara (Akihabara Sta.)

Tokyo Disneyland
東京ディズニーランド
tookyoo dizunii-rando (Maihama Sta.)

Kabuki-za Theater
歌舞伎座
kabuki-za (Higashi-Ginza Sta.)

Tsukiji Fish Market
築地
tsukiji (Tsukiji Sta.)

Odaiba amusement district
お台場
odaiba (Daiba Sta.)

** Tokyo is an action-packed city and there is something for everyone. If you can't find anything interesting to do or see in Tokyo, you're better off at home! （東京はイベント満載な街。えっ、何も気に入った物が見つからない？ 帰んなさい！）

Japan Highlights 1
横浜・大阪・京都・広島
Yokomaha, Osaka, Kyoto, Hiroshima

Yokohama
横浜
yokohama

like
好き
suki

Yamashita(-koen) Park
山下公園
yamashita koo'en

Yokohama Chinatown
横浜中華街
yokohama chuuka-gai

Yokosuka
(Japanese/U.S. navy bases)
横須賀
yokosuka

the Great Buddha of Kamakura
鎌倉大仏
kamakura daibutsu

Kencho-ji Zen Temple
建長寺
kenchoo-ji

Osaka
大阪
oosaka

love
大好き
dai-suki

Osaka Castle
大阪城
oosaka-joo

Dotonbori
道頓堀
dootom-bori

Koshien Stadium
甲子園球場
kooshi'en kyuujoo
(in Hyogo Prefecture)

*Tako-yaki
たこ焼き
fried octopus dumplings

Kansai International Airport
関西国際空港
kansai kokusai kuukoo

---

(24) * Osaka is well-known for its fine restaurants and is called "the Town of Overeating." Some of the restaurants have moving mascots on their billboards. (食べ物の美味しい大阪は「食い倒れの街」と呼ばれ、動く看板つきのレストランもある)

Geography 地理

Japan Highlights 1

Kyoto 京都 *kyooto*

beautiful 美しい *utsukushii*

Nishi Hongan-ji Temple 西本願寺 *nishi hongan-ji*

Kiyomizu-dera Temple 清水寺 *kiyomizu-dera*

Maruyama(-koen) Park 円山公園 *maruyama kooen*

Gion Entertainment District 祇園 *gion*

Geisha / Maiko 芸者 / 舞妓 *geesha / maiko*

Kyoto cuisine 京料理 *kyoo ryoori*

** (final-year) school trip 修学旅行 *shuugaku-ryokoo*

Hiroshima 広島 *hiroshima*

unique 個性的 *kosee-teki*

Atomic Bomb Dome 原爆ドーム *gembaku doomu*

Peace Memorial Park 平和記念公園 *heewa kinen koo'en*

Miyajima 宮島 *miyajima*

** Kyoto is popular for school trips. International tourists might marvel more at the sheer number of kids in uniform than at Kyoto's cultural treasures. 修学旅行に人気の京都。海外からの旅行者は建造物よりも修学旅行に来た生徒の多さに驚くかも）

Japan Highlights 2

九州・沖縄・東北・北海道
Kyushu, Okinawa, Tohoku, Hokkaido

九州・沖縄・東北・北海道

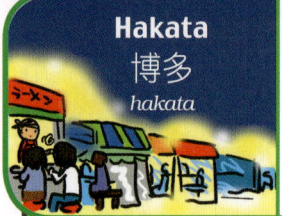

Hakata
博多
hakata

fun/enjoyable
楽しい
tanoshii

Hakata Dontaku Festival
博多どんたく
hakata dontaku

Dazai-fu (old capital of Kyushu)
太宰府
dazai-fu

Hakata Raamen
博多ラーメン
Chinese-style noodles in savory pork broth

Nagasaki
長崎
nagasaki

exotic
異国風
ikoku-fuu

Nagasaki Peace Park
長崎平和公園
nagasaki heewa koo'en

Okinawa
沖縄
okinawa

interesting
面白い
omoshiroi

Anti-war Monument of Himeyuri
ひめゆりの塔
himeyuri no too

Shiisa (Okinawan lion ornament)
シーサー
shiisaa

Kokusai-dori Blvd. in Naha
那覇 国際通り
naha kokusai-doori

* **Gooyaa Champuruu**
ゴーヤーチャンプルー
bitter gourd pan-fried with tofu and egg

Awamori
泡盛
Okinawan-style rice liquor

* Okinawan food is very healthy and may explain why people there live longer than anywhere else in Japan. Bitter gourd, for example, helps cleanse the bloodstream. (沖縄の食べ物は長寿食。ゴーヤーにも血液の浄化作用がある)

Geography 地理

Japan Highlights 2

Tohoku Region
東北
toohoku → P.18

trying their best / toughing it out
がんばってる
gambatteru

Nebuta Lantern Float Festival
ねぶた祭り
nebuta matsuri

Kanto Lantern Pole Festival
竿灯祭り
kantoo matsuri

Sendai Star Festival
仙台七夕祭り
sendai tanabata matsuri

2011 Great East Japan Earthquake
東日本大震災
higashi nihon dai-shinsai

Thank you for your support.

restoration effort **
復興努力
fukkoo doryoku

Hokkaido
北海道
hokkaidoo

great
すごい
sugoi

Sapporo Snow Festival
札幌雪祭り
sapporo yuki matsuri

Kushiro Marshlands (national park)
釧路湿原
kushiro shitsugen

Susukino Entertainment District
ススキノ
susukino

Yubari Melon
夕張メロン
yuubari meron

"Genghis-Khan" lamb barbecue
ジンギスカン料理
Hokkaido-style lamb and vegetable barbecue

** I want to thank every one of you who has extended a helping hand. Thank you so much for letting us know that you care. (日本のことを思い、手を差し伸べてくださったみなさん、本当にありがとう)

Manners & Customs
礼儀と習慣
reegi to shuukan

| Please tell /teach me. 教えてください *oshi'ete kudasai* | (social) customs 習慣 *shuukan* | manners マナー *manaa* | social etiquette 礼儀 *reegi* |

礼儀と習慣

bowing
お辞儀
ojigi

avoiding long eye contact
目を合わせ過ぎない
me o awase-sugi-nai

taking off your shoes
靴を脱ぐ
kutsu o nugu

"proper" Japanese sitting posture
正座
seeza

diplomatic show of interest, concern, appreciation, etc.
建前
tatema'e

real intention, feelings, etc.
本音
hon'ne

gift-giving
贈り物
okurimono

giving something back
お返し
oka'eshi

souvenir
おみやげ
omiyage

It's only a small gift.
つまらない物ですが
tsumara-nai mono des ga

*What a nice gift!
結構なものを
kekkoo-na mono o

Just a little thank-you gift.
ほんのお返しです
hon'no oka'eshi des

* Another popular response is "doomo sumimasen." More than just the equivalent of "Excuse me." it is also used for apologies and to express gratitude. (代わりに「どうもすみません」という言葉で、感謝や謝罪の気持ちを伝えることもある)

Life in Japan 生活

Manners & Customs

senior/older 目上 me-u'e 	**junior / younger** 目下 me-shita 	**older/more experienced** 先輩 sempai	**younger/less experienced** 後輩 koohai
thoughtful attention 気配り kikubari	**flattery** お世辞 oseji 	** **respectful language** 敬語 keego	**talk behind someone's back** 陰口 kage-guchi 
unity/harmony 和 wa 	**clique / faction** 派閥 habatsu 	**pride/face** 面目 memboku	**shame** 恥 haji 
reserve/restraint 遠慮 enryo 	**modesty** 謙遜 kenson 	**patience** 我慢 gaman 	**trying your best/ toughing it out** 頑張る gambaru
social obligation 義理 giri	**warmth/ kindness** 人情 ninjoo	**personal connection** コネ kone	**name cards** 名刺 meeshi 

do's and don'ts on trains and buses 車内マナー shanai manaa 	**Do not jump the line.** 列に割り込まない retsu ni warikoma-nai	**No smoking.** 禁煙 kin'en
Refrain from talking on the phone. 通話は控える tsuuwa wa hika'eru	**mutual courtesy and respect** お互いへの気遣い otagai e no kizukai	**priority seats** 優先席 yuusen seki 

* * In Japan young people are expected to be polite and respectful toward seniors. That's why "polite" people waste no time in asking your age. (日本では年下の人が気を遣う習慣があるため、丁寧な人ほどすぐに年齢を尋ねたりする)

29

Introducing Yourself 自己紹介 jiko-shookai

How do you do?
はじめまして
hajime-mashite

My name is 〜.
私の名前は〜（です）
watashi no nama'e wa 〜 (des)

自己紹介

Nice to meet you. よろしく（お願いします） yoroshiku (onegai shimas)	**Nice to meet you, too.** こちらこそ kochira-koso
And your name is…? （すみません）お名前は？ (sumimasen) o-nama'e wa	**Nice meeting you.** 今後ともよろしく（お願いします） kongo-tomo yoroshiku (onegai shimas)
* **I appreciate your help.** お世話になります osewa ni narimas	**Thank you for your kindness.** いつもすみません itsumo sumimasen

Noriko-san ノリコさん being polite (universal)	**Noriko-chan** ノリコちゃん being friendly (esp. for girls)	**Yamada-san** 山田さん showing respect (for seniors/superiors)	**Yamada-kun** 山田君 showing friendliness (for juniors/subordinates)

 **I can speak.** 話せます hanase-mas	**I can't speak.** 話せません hanase-masen	**Can you speak?** 話せますか？ hanase-mas-ka	**I am learning.** 勉強中（です） benkyoo-chuu (des)

Japanese 日本語 nihon-go	**English** 英語 eego	**Korean** 韓国語 kankoku-go	**Chinese** 中国語 chuugoku-go	**Thai** タイ語 tai-go

Tagalog タガログ語 tagarogu-go	**Malay** マレー語 maree-go	**Vietnamese** ベトナム語 betonamu-go	**Indonesian** インドネシア語 indonesia-go

* A diplomatic phrase with no English equivalent, it literally means "I appreciate your looking after me." Say it when you move in, meet your new boss and co-workers, etc. (「お世話になります」にピッタリの英訳はない)

Life in Japan　生活

I am from ～.
～から来ました
~kara kimashita

I was born in ～.
～生まれ（です）
~umare (des)

Where are you from?
（ご）出身は？
(go) shusshin wa

What part of the country?
どこの地方（ですか）？
doko no chihoo (des-ka)

What kind of place is it?
どんな所（ですか）？
don'na tokoro (des-ka)

What is it famous for?
何が有名（ですか）？
nani ga yuumee des-ka

Introducing Yourself

I have been there.
行ったことあります
itta koto arimas

Have you been there?
行ったことありますか？
itta koto arimas-ka

I haven't been there.
行ったことありません
itta koto arimasen

U.S.A. アメリカ *amerika*	**Britain** 英国／イギリス *eekoku/igirisu*	**Australia** オーストラリア *oosuto-raria*	**New Zealand** ニュージーランド *nyuujii-rando*

Canada カナダ *kanada*	**Malaysia** マレーシア *mareeshia*	**Vietnam** ベトナム *betonamu*	**Indonesia** インドネシア *indoneshia*

South Korea 韓国 *kankoku*	**China** 中国 *chuugoku*	**Taiwan** 台湾 *taiwan*	**Thailand** タイ *tai*
Phillipines フィリピン *firipin*	**Singapore** シンガポール *shinga-pooru*	**Hong Kong** 香港 *honkon*	**Japan** 日本 *nihon/nippon*

→ P.18.

Older Japanese may upset you by asking very personal questions. Whether you like it or not, they ask such questions only to those they want to be friends with. （年配の日本人は、気に入った人ほど、個人的な質問をして困らせがちだ）

Hobbies & Friends 趣味と友だち
shumi to tomodachi

* **What are your hobbies?** 趣味は（何ですか）？ *shumi wa (nan des-ka)*	**What do you like?** 何が好き（ですか）？ *nani ga suki (des-ka)*

趣味と友だち

music 音楽 *ongaku*	**movies** 映画 *eega*	**cartoons** アニメ *anime* 	**TV** テレビ *terebi*
going downtown 街歩き *machi-aruki*	**eating out** 食べ歩き *tabe-aruki* 	**fashion/ dressing up** おしゃれ *oshare* 	**shopping** 買い物 *kaimono* 
travel 旅行 *ryokoo*	**driving** ドライブ *doraibu*	**fishing** 釣り *tsuri*	**outdoor activities** アウトドア *a'uto-do'a* 
photography 写真 *shashin*	**theater/acting** 演劇 *engeki* 	**computers** パソコン *pasokon*	**writing emails** メール *meeru*
karaoke カラオケ *kara'oke*	**drinking** 酒 *sake* 	**"blind date" party** 合コン *gookon* 	**(watching) DVDs** DVD *dii bui dii*
painting/ drawing 絵 *e* 	**video games** コンピューターゲーム *kompyuutaa geemu*	**cooking** 料理 *ryoori* 	**chatting** おしゃべり *oshaberi*
fortune-telling 占い *uranai* 	**manga comic books** 漫画 *manga* 	**reading** 読書 *dokusho*	**sports** スポーツ *supootsu* 
gambling ギャンブル *gyamburu*	**horse racing** 競馬 *keeba*	**Pachinko** パチンコ *pachinko* 	**cafés** カフェ *kafe*

* The word "shumi" translates as either "hobby" or "pastime." Don't be surprised if someone says their "shumi" is sleeping (「趣味」という日本語の定義は結構曖昧。「趣味」を「寝る事」と答える人もいるが呆れないように).

Life in Japan 生活

What kind of person?
どんな人？
don'na hito

I / me 私 watashi

you あなた anata

| man/male 男性 dansee | he 彼 kare  | woman/female 女性 josee  | she 彼女 kanojo |

rich お金持ち okane-mochi 	poor ビンボー bimboo 	generous 気前がいい kima'e ga ii 	stingy ケチ kechi 
cool カッコいい kakko-ii	uncool ダサイ dasai	cute カワイイ kawa'ii	ugly ブサイク busaiku
trustworthy/serious 真面目 majime	untrustworthy いい加減 ii-kagen	nice/sympathetic 優しい yasashii	mean 意地悪 ijiwaru
exciting/fun 楽しい tanoshii	boring つまらない tsumaranai	funny/interesting 面白い omoshiroi	weird/strange おかしい okashii
talkative おしゃべり oshaberi	quiet 大人しい otonashii	smart 頭いい atama-ii	stupid バカ baka
hasty/impatient せっかち sekkachi	laidback のんびり nombiri	sexually naughty やらしい yarashii	irritating ムカつく mukatsuku
selfish わがまま wagamama	good-looking 美形 bikee	shy 照れ屋 tereya	moody 気分屋 kibun'ya

Hobbies & Friends

Japanese people think it's impolite to tell an "unkind truth." Words like "chotto" and "nee" are signs that you should stop pressing for an answer. (日本人は言いづらい事を言うのが苦手。「ちょっと」や「ねぇ…」で言葉を濁しだしたら突っ込まない)

Work & School 仕事と勉強 *shigoto to benkyoo*

What do you do?
（お）仕事は何ですか？
(o-)shigoto wa nan des-ka

* **Which company do you work for?**
どちらの会社ですか？
dochira no kaisha des-ka

仕事と勉強

office worker (male) サラリーマン *sararii-man*	office worker (female) ＯＬ *oo'eru*	middle manager 中間管理職 *chuukan kanri-shoku*	manager 管理職 *kanri-shoku*
full-time worker 正社員 *see-shain*	contract worker 契約社員 *keeyaku-shain*	temp 派遣社員 *haken-shain*	casual worker フリーター *furiitaa*
sales 営業 *eegyoo*	administration 総務 *soomu*	accounting 経理 *keeri*	engineer(ing) エンジニア *enjinia*	secretary 秘書 *hisho*

delivery 運送 *unsoo* 	food 食品 *shokuhin*	advertising 広告 *kookoku*	information technology IT 関係 *ai tii kankee*
public servant 公務員 *koomuin*	medical 医療 *iryoo*	apparel アパレル *apareru* 	publishing 出版 *shuppan*
agriculture 農業 *noogyoo*	service industry サービス業 *saabisu-gyoo*	manufacturing 製造業 *seezoo-gyoo*	education 教育 *kyoo'iku*
printing 印刷 *insatsu*	finance 金融 *kin'yuu*	mass media マスコミ *masukomi*	show business 芸能 *gee'noo*

laid off リストラ *risutora*	unemployed 失業中 *shitsugyoo-chuu*	looking for a job 求職中 *kyuushoku-chuu* 	retired *(and living on a pension)* 年金生活 *nenkin seekatsu*

* Japanese usually talk about their work in terms of their company rather than what they do for a living. Not many can explain the content of their work in English very well. (日本では職種よりも社名。英語で職種を聞くと、しどろもどろな人も多い)

Life in Japan 生活

student 学生 *gakusee* 	pupil 生徒 *seeto* 	** Where do you go to school? どちらの学校ですか？ *dochira no gakkoo des-ka* 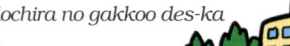

kindergarten 幼稚園 *yoochi'en*	elementary school 小学校 *shoo-gakkoo*	junior high school 中学校 *chuu-gakkoo* 	high school 高校 *kookoo* 
vocational college 専門学校 *sem'mon-gakkoo*	junior college 短大 *tandai* 	university 大学 *daigaku*	graduate school 大学院 *daigaku-in*

Work & School

I like 好き *suki*	I dislike/hate 嫌い *kirai*	good/ strong (at) 得意 *tokui*	weak/poor (at) 苦手 *nigate* 
arithmetic 算数 *sansuu*	math 数学 *suugaku*	Japanese 日本語/国語 *nihon-go/kokugo* 	English 英語 *eego*
music 音楽 *ongaku* 	science 科学 *kagaku*	chemistry 化学 *kagaku*	physics 物理 *butsuri*
social studies 社会 *shakai*	geography 地理 *chiri* 	history 歴史 *rekishi*	economics 経済 *keezai*
art 美術 *bijutsu*	home economics 家庭科 *katee-ka*	industrial arts 技術科 *gijutsu-ka* 	sports 体育 *ta'i'iku* 

work part-time アルバイト *arubaito*	looking for a (full-time) job 就職活動中 *shuushoku katudoo-chuu*	preparing for an entrance exam 受験勉強中 *juken benkyoo-chuu*	want to study abroad 留学したい *ryuugaku shitai* 

** Despite the increasing number of suicides among "company men", the myth survives that a good school and a good company lead to a good life. (会社人間の自殺が増えても、有名校から一流企業に入れば幸せになれるという「神話」はしぶとく生き続ける)

Money & Numbers お金と数字
okane to suuji

How much?	Please write it down.	change	sales tax
いくら（ですか）？	書いて下さい	おつり	消費税
ikura (des-ka)	kaite kudasai	otsuri	shoohi-zee

10,000 yen	5,000 yen	2,000 yen	1,000 yen
１万円	５千円	２千円	千円
ichi-man en	go-sen en	ni-sen en	sen en
		 * now a rarity	

500 yen	100 yen	50 yen	10 yen
500 円 	100 円 	50 円 	10 円 
go-hyaku en	hyaku en	go-juu en	juu en

5 yen	1 yen		* Please break my bill.
５円 	１円		両替して下さい
go en	ichi en		ryooga'e shite kudasai

Please exchange my money.	bank	currency exchange
両替して下さい	銀行	両替所
ryooga'e shite kudasai	ginkoo	ryooga'e-jo

What's the exchange rate?	yen	won	euro
レートはいくら？	円	ウォン	ユーロ
reeto wa ikura?	en	won	yuuro

dollar	Which country?		yuan	pound
ドル	どこのドル		元	ポンド
doru	doko no doru?	MEMO	gen	pondo

payment	cash	credit card	duty-free/tax-free
支払い	現金	クレジットカード	免税
shiharai	genkin	kurejitto kaado	menzee

* Shops that refuse to give small change to non-customers have one thing in common: a "Japlish" sign that says "NO EXCHANGE." (両替を嫌がる店ほど、「NO EXCHANGE（品物の交換お断り）」というわかりにくい日本人英語の張り紙がある。)

Shopping 数字・買い物

Please teach/show me.
教えて下さい
oshi'ete kudasai

How many?
いくつ
ikutsu

some
すこし
sukoshi

many/much
たくさん
takusan

I don't know how to say it.
言い方がわかりません
ii kata ga wakari-masen

I'll write it down.
書きます
kaki-masu

Money & Numbers

English	Japanese	Romaji
open a bank account	口座を開く	kooza o hiraku
withdraw money **	引き出す	hikidasu
deposite money	預金する	yokin suru
check the balance	残高照会	zandaka shookai
update bankbook	通帳記入	tsuuchoo ki'nyuu
make payment	振り込む	furikomu
recipient of payment	振り込み先	furikomi-saki
account number	口座番号	kooza bangoo

zero 0 *zero*		
one 1 *ichi*	eleven 11 *juu-ichi*	
two 2 *ni*	twelve 12 *juu-ni*	
three 3 *san*	thirteen 13 *juu-san*	thirty 30 *san-juu*
four 4 *yon*	fourteen 14 *juu-yon*	forty 40 *yon-juu*
five 5 *go*	fifteen 15 *juu-go*	fifty 50 *go-juu*
six 6 *roku*	sixteen 16 *juu-roku*	sixty 60 *roku-juu*
seven 7 *nana*	seventeen 17 *juu-nana*	seventy 70 *nana-juu*
eight 8 *hachi*	eighteen 18 *juu-hachi*	eighty 80 *hachi-juu*
nine 9 *kyuu*	nineteen 19 *juu-kyuu*	ninety 90 *kyuu-juu*
ten 10 *juu*	twenty 20 *ni-juu*	one hundred 100 *hyaku*

** Major banks in Japan now have ATMs at most convenience stores. Check to see if your nearest "convenience ATM" has your bank logo. (日本の有名銀行のカードがあれば、コンビニのATMからでも引き出しが可能になった)

Clothes & Colors 服と色 *fuku to iro*

I want ~. (~が) 欲しい *(~ga) hoshii*	**How much?** いくら（ですか）？ *ikura (des-ka)*
	Just looking, thanks. 見てるだけ（です） *miteru dake (des)*

men's 男物 *otoko-mono*	**ladies'** 女物 *on'na-mono* 	**Which one is popular?** どれが人気（ですか）？ *dore ga ninki (des-ka)*

shirt シャツ *shatsu* 	**T-shirt** Tシャツ *tii shatsu* 	**business shirt** Yシャツ *wai shatsu* 	**blouse** ブラウス *buraasu* 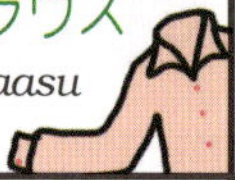	**sweater** セーター *seetaa* 
long sleeves 長袖 *naga-sode* 	**short sleeves** 半袖 *han-sode* 	**sleeveless** ノースリーブ *noo-suriibu* 	**parka** パーカ *paaka* 	**track suit** ジャージ *jaaji* 
business jacket ジャケット *jaketto* 	**business suit** スーツ *suutsu* 	**necktie** ネクタイ *nekutai* 	**coat** コート *kooto* 	**hat/cap** 帽子 *booshi* 
trousers ズボン *zubon* 	**jeans** ジーンズ *jiinzu* 	**skirt** スカート *sukaato* 	**zip-up jacket** ジャンパー *jampaa* 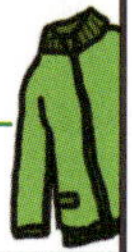	**pajamas** パジャマ *pajama* 
underwear 下着 *shitagi* 	**underpants** パンツ *pantsu* 	**bra** ブラ *bura* 	**panties** パンティー *pantii* 	**panty hose** パンスト *pansuto* 
swimsuit 水着 *mizugi* 	**handkerchief** ハンカチ *hankachi* 	**belt** ベルト *beruto* 	**socks** 靴下 *kutsu-shita* 	**shoes** 靴 *kutsu* 

服と色

* Many of the latest fashion words are borrowed words from English. Try saying them very slowly. They will likely understand you. （最近のファッション用語には英語が多いため、ゆっくり言えば英語のまま理解してもらえる場合もある）

Shopping 数字・買い物

Can I try it on?
試着していい（ですか）？
shichaku shite ii (des-ka)

I'll take it.
これにします
kore ni shimas

No thanks.
やめます
yamemas

Do you (they) have ~?
~ありますか？
~ arimas-ka

bigger
もっと大きいの
motto ookii no

smaller
もっと小さいの
motto chiisai no

different color **
ちがう色
chiga'u iro

different pattern
ちがう柄
chiga'u gara

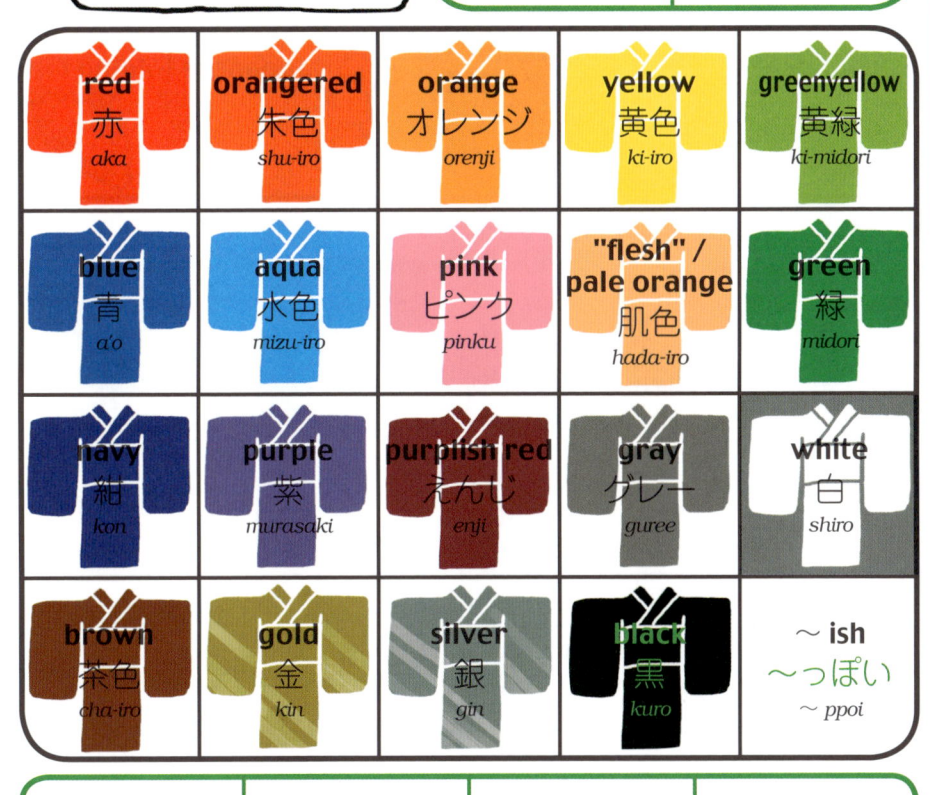

Clothes & Colors

red 赤 *aka*	**orangered** 朱色 *shu-iro*	**orange** オレンジ *orenji*	**yellow** 黄色 *ki-iro*	**greenyellow** 黄緑 *ki-midori*
blue 青 *a'o*	**aqua** 水色 *mizu-iro*	**pink** ピンク *pinku*	**"flesh" / pale orange** 肌色 *hada-iro*	**green** 緑 *midori*
navy 紺 *kon*	**purple** 紫 *murasaki*	**purplish red** えんじ *enji*	**gray** グレー *guree*	**white** 白 *shiro*
brown 茶色 *cha-iro*	**gold** 金 *kin*	**silver** 銀 *gin*	**black** 黒 *kuro*	**~ ish** ~っぽい *~ ppoi*

looks good
似合う
ni'a'u

doesn't look good
似合わない
ni'awa-nai

loud/colorful
派手
hade

plain/subdued
地味
jimi

** Ironically, the very colors foreigners find fascinating in things traditionally Japanese don't have corresponding English names. (皮肉なことに、外国人が魅力を感じる日本の色ほど、英語名はついていなかったりする)

Souvenirs of Japan おみやげ *omiyage*

I'm looking for 〜．
（〜を）探しています
(~o)sagashite-imas

Where can I buy?
どこで買えますか？
doko de ka'emas-ka

souvenir おみやげ *omiyage*	for men 男性向き *dansee-muki*	for children 子供向き *kodomo-muki*	local favorite 地元で人気 *jimoto de ninki*
gift 贈り物 *okurimono*	for women 女性向き *josee-muki*	for young people 若者向き *wakamono-muki*	your recommendation あなたのおすすめ *anata no osusume*

おみやげ

Japanese doll 日本人形 *nihon ningyoo*	"Kokeshi" wooden doll こけし *kokeshi*		Japanese folding fan 扇子 *sensu*
informal Kimono for summer 浴衣 *yukata*	Happi coat はっぴ *happi*		lacqureware 塗り物 *nurimono*
"Ukiyoe" print 浮世絵 *ukiyo'e*	Japanese monochrome painting 水墨画 *suibokuga*	pottery/chinaware 焼き物 *yakimono*	good-luck charm お守り *omamori*
Japanese traditional kite 和凧 *wadako*	Japanese traditional wooden racket 羽子板 *hagoita*	Japanese traditional comb 櫛 *kushi*	good-luck "beckoning" cat doll * 招き猫 *maneki-neko*
wooden clogs 下駄 *geta*	handicraft 民芸品 *mingee-hin*	wind chime 風鈴 *fuurin*	postcard 絵葉書 *ehagaki*

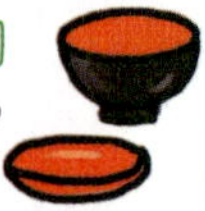

40　＊ Even "maneki-neko" dolls have color variations in kitschy Japan. You'll see black, gold and even pink ones, but the traditional color is good old white. (最近では招き猫もカラフルになってきたが、本流はやはり昔ながらの白だ)

Shopping 数字・買い物

Souvenirs of Japan

Japanese teapot 急須 kyuusu	Japanese wrapping cloth 風呂敷 furoshiki	chopsticks 箸 hashi
Japanese character T-shirt 日本語Tシャツ nihon-go tii-shatsu	Anime goods アニメグッズ anime guzzu	** celebrity collectibles タレントグッズ tarento guzzu
books on Japan 日本の本 nihon no hon	books on Japanese language 日本語の本 nihon-go no hon	books on Japanese food 日本料理の本 nihon ryoori no hon
"Gashapon" capsule toys ガシャポンのグッズ gashapon no guzzu	comic books まんが manga	ninja/samurai toys and souvenirs 時代劇グッズ jidaigeki guzzu

This is a gift. プレゼント用です purezento-yoo des	Please wrap it. 包んで下さい tsutsunde kudasai	Make sure it won't break. 壊れないように koware-nai yooni
Is it duty-free / tax-free? 免税ですか？ menzee des-ka	Please lower the price. 安くして下さい yasuku shite kudasai	Please give me a little extra for free. おまけして下さい omake shite kudasai

Please send it.
送って下さい
okutte kudasai

How much? いくら？ ikura	postage 送料 sooryoo	insurance 保険 hoken
recipient 送り先 okuri-saki	address 住所 juusho	telephone 電話 den'wa

** Celebrity collectibles are big business in Japan. But once the celebrities themselves are forgotten, collectibles become more a source of amusement than antiques.（タレントが過去の人になると、グッズは笑いのネタになりがちである）

Daily Necessities
雑貨・電化製品
zakka / denka-seehin

Where can I buy?
どこで買えますか？
doko de ka'emas-ka

Bic Camera	Yodobashi Camera
ビックカメラ	ヨドバシカメラ
bikku kamera	*yodobashi camera*

メモ	supermarket	electric appliance store *
MEMO	スーパー	電気屋
	suupaa	*denki-ya*

雑貨・電化製品

personal computer	computer supplies	smartphone	calculator
パソコン	パソコン用品	スマートフォン	計算機
paso-kon	*paso-kon yoohin*	*smaato-fon*	*keesan-ki*
hair drier	iPod	rice cooker	mobile phone strap
ドライヤー	iPod	炊飯器	携帯ストラップ
doraiyaa	*ai-poddo*	*suihan-ki*	*keetai sutorappu*
headphones	adapter	digital camera	digital audio player
ヘッドフォン	アダプター	デジカメ	デジタルオーディオプレーヤー
heddo-fon	*adaputaa*	*deji-kame*	*dejitaru oodio pureeyaa*
alarm clock	transformer	camcorder	memory card
目覚まし時計	変圧器	ビデオカメラ	メモリーカード
mezamashi-dokei	*hen'atsu-ki*	*bideo-kamera*	*memorii kaado*
facial care products	blank DVDs	wristwatch	SIM card
フェイスケア用品	DVDメディア	腕時計	SIM カード
feesu ke'a yoohin	*dii bui dii media*	*ude-dokee*	*shimu kaado*

battery	D/C	AA/AAA	I want ~like this(these).
電池	単1／単2	単3／単4	これと同じの下さい
denchi	*tan-ichi/tan-ni*	*tan-san/tan-yon*	*kore to onaji no kudasai*

* If you're in the suburbs, look for Kojima or K's Denki. These stores offer a large selection of electric appliances at very low prices.（都市部以外では、コジマやケーズデンキを探してみよう。品揃え豊富で安く、あなどれないぞ）

Shopping 数字・買い物

convenience store コンビニ *kombini*	**drugstore** 薬局 *yakkyoku*	**** 100-yen shop** 100円ショップ *hyaku-en shoppu*	**variety shop** 雑貨屋 *zakka-ya*

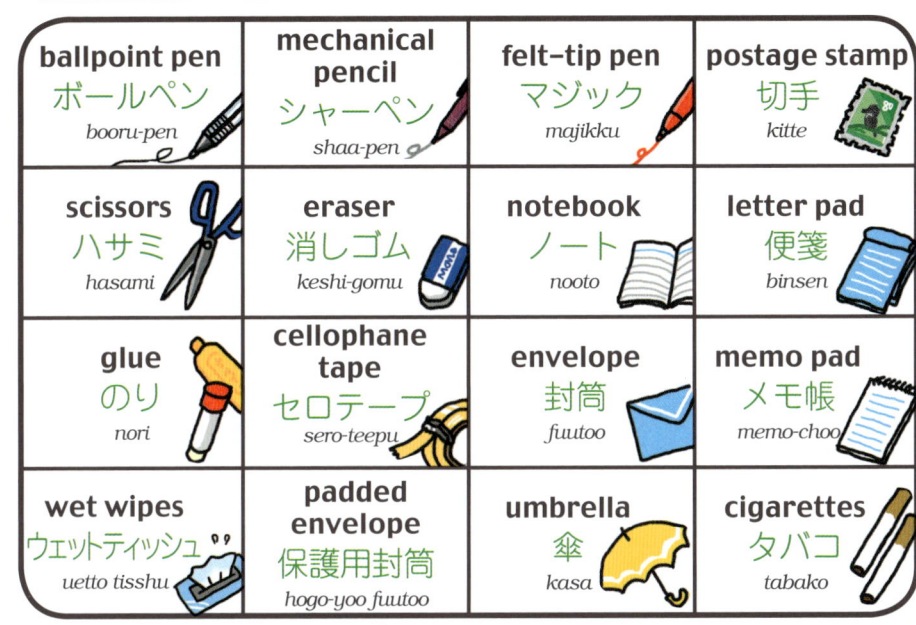

Daily Necessities

ballpoint pen ボールペン *booru-pen*	**mechanical pencil** シャーペン *shaa-pen*	**felt-tip pen** マジック *majikku*	**postage stamp** 切手 *kitte*
scissors ハサミ *hasami*	**eraser** 消しゴム *keshi-gomu*	**notebook** ノート *nooto*	**letter pad** 便箋 *binsen*
glue のり *nori*	**cellophane tape** セロテープ *sero-teepu*	**envelope** 封筒 *fuutoo*	**memo pad** メモ帳 *memo-choo*
wet wipes ウェットティッシュ *uetto tisshu*	**padded envelope** 保護用封筒 *hogo-yoo fuutoo*	**umbrella** 傘 *kasa*	**cigarettes** タバコ *tabako*

detergent 洗剤 *senzai*	**soap** 石鹸 *sekken*	**towel** タオル *ta'oru*	**razor** カミソリ *kamisori*	**men's/ladies'** 男性用／女性用 *dansee-yoo/josee-yoo*
toothbrush 歯ブラシ *haburashi*	**toothpaste** 歯みがき *hamigaki*	**tissues** ティッシュ *tisshu*	**toilet paper** トイレットペーパー *toiretto-peepaa*	**nail clippers** つめ切り *tsume-kiri*
hair brush ヘアブラシ *he'a-burashi*	**shampoo** シャンプー *shampuu*	**conditioner** リンス *rinsu*	**cotton swabs** 綿棒 *memboo*	**slippers** スリッパ *surippa*
perfume 香水 *koo-sui*	**hair products** ヘア用品 *he'a yoohin*	**cosmetics** 化粧品 *keshoo-hin*	**sanitary products** 生理用品 *seeri yoohin*	**condoms** コンドーム *kondoomu*

** Daiso is the name of a 100-yen "department store" where you can buy everything from calculators to underwear for 100 yen each. (ダイソーは百貨店級の品揃えの100円ショップ。計算機から下着類までみな100円で買える)

Shops in Your Town
コンビニ・商店街
kombini / shooten-gai

Where is ～? どこにありますか？ *doko ni arimas-ka* → P.12	convenience store コンビニ *kombini*	supermarket スーパー *suupaa*

convenience store

Seven Eleven セブンイレブン *sebun irebun*	Lawson ローソン *rooson*	Family Mart ファミリーマート *famirii maato*
NEWDAYS NEWDAYS *nyuu-deizu*	Circle K /Sunkus サークルK／サンクス *saakuru kee / sankusu*	Mini Stop ミニストップ *mini sutoppu*

boxed lunch お弁当 *obentoo*	side dish おかず *okazu*	(Please) heat it. 温めて（下さい） *atatamete (kudasai)*

chopsticks 箸 *hashi*	spoon スプーン *supuun*	fork フォーク *fooku*	straw ストロー *sutoroo*	Please (give me). 下さい *kudasai*

supermarket

Daiei ダイエー *daiee*	Ito Yokado イトーヨーカドー *itoo yookadoo*	AEON イオン *ion*
Seiyu 西友 *seeyuu*	MaxValu マックスバリュ *makkusu baryu*	Inageya いなげや *inage-ya*

Which floor? 何階（ですか）？ *nan-kai (des-ka)*	groceries → P.37 食料品＊ *shokuryoo-hin*	clothing → P.62 衣料品 *iryoo-hin* → P.38

＊ You'll usually find the grocery section in the basement (chika). Between 6 and 7 p.m. they usually have a red-light sale to get rid of leftover Sushi. (食料品は通常地下にあり、夕方6～7時頃に売れ残りの寿司の叩き売りがあることが多い)

Shopping 数字・買い物

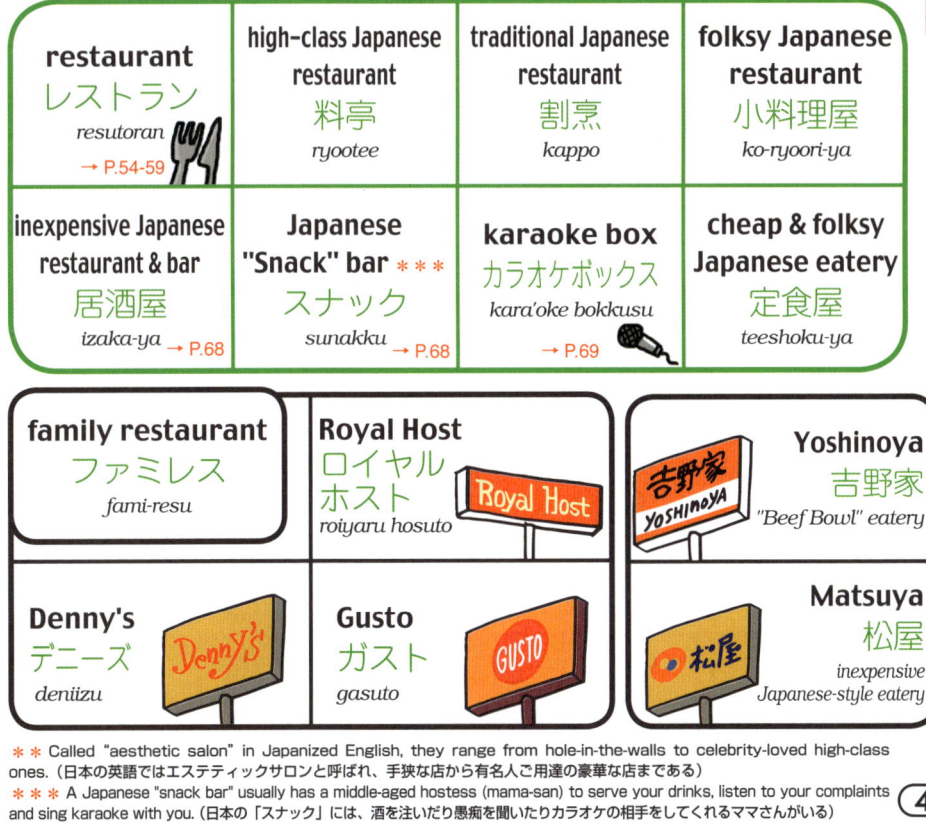

Shops in Your Town

shop(s) 店 mise	**meat shop** → P.65 肉屋 niku-ya	**vegetable shop** → P.62 八百屋 ya'o-ya	**fruit shop** → P.62 果物屋 kudamono-ya
bakery パン屋 pan-ya	**liquor shop** → P.67 酒屋 saka-ya	**variety shop** → P.43 雑貨屋 zakka-ya	**100-yen shop** → P.43 100円ショップ hyaku-en shoppu
barbershop → P.83 床屋 toko-ya	**hair salon** → P.83 美容院 biyoo'in	**clothing shop** → P.38 洋品店 yoohin-ten	**boutique** → P.38 ブティック butikku
drugstore → P.74 薬局 yakkyoku	**✶✶ day spa** エステ esute	**optometrist** 眼鏡屋 megane-ya	**CD shop** CDショップ shii dii shoppu

restaurant レストラン resutoran → P.54-59	**high-class Japanese restaurant** 料亭 ryootee	**traditional Japanese restaurant** 割烹 kappo	**folksy Japanese restaurant** 小料理屋 ko-ryoori-ya
inexpensive Japanese restaurant & bar 居酒屋 izaka-ya → P.68	**Japanese "Snack" bar** ✶✶✶ スナック sunakku → P.68	**karaoke box** カラオケボックス kara'oke bokkusu → P.69	**cheap & folksy Japanese eatery** 定食屋 teeshoku-ya

family restaurant ファミレス fami-resu	**Royal Host** ロイヤルホスト roiyaru hosuto		**Yoshinoya** 吉野家 "Beef Bowl" eatery
Denny's デニーズ deniizu	**Gusto** ガスト gasuto		**Matsuya** 松屋 inexpensive Japanese-style eatery

✶✶ Called "aesthetic salon" in Japanized English, they range from hole-in-the-walls to celebrity-loved high-class ones. (日本の英語ではエステティックサロンと呼ばれ、手狭な店から有名人ご用達の豪華な店まである)

✶✶✶ A Japanese "snack bar" usually has a middle-aged hostess (mama-san) to serve your drinks, listen to your complaints and sing karaoke with you. (日本の「スナック」には、酒を注いだり愚痴を聞いたりカラオケの相手をしてくれるママさんがいる)

Japanese Calendar
一年と天気 ichi-nen to tenki

* Christmas Eve
クリスマスイブ
(Dec. 24)
kurisumasu ibu

Soba Noodles Eating on New Year's Eve
年越しそば
toshi-koshi soba

Celebration for 7, 5 & 3-Year-Olds
七五三
(Nov. 15)
shichi-go-san

year-end party
忘年会
(early - late December)
boonen-kai

year-end house cleaning
大掃除
(late December)
oo-sooji

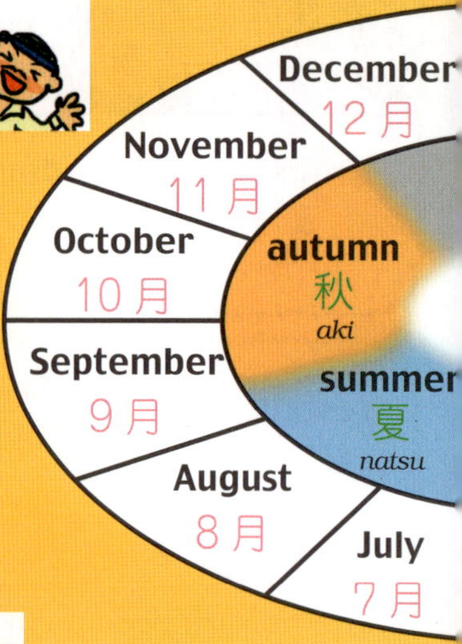

school festival season
学園祭
(late October - early November)
gaku'en-sai

typhoon season
台風シーズン
(September)
taifuu shiizun

December 12月
November 11月
October 10月
September 9月
August 8月
July 7月

autumn 秋 aki
summer 夏 natsu

Equinoctial Visit to Family Grave
お彼岸
(mid March/mid September)
ohigan

"Obon" Buddhist Festival
お盆
(mid July/mid August)
obon

climate
気候
kikoo

hot 暑い atsui	**nice/mild** 過ごしやすい sugoshi-yasui
humid (& hot) 蒸し暑い mushi-atsui	**cool** 涼しい suzushii
warm (& nice) 暖かい atatakai	**cold** 寒い samui

fireworks shows
花火大会
(mid July-late August)
hanabi taikai

Star Festival
七夕
(July 7)
tanabata

一年と天気

46　* Christmas Eve in Japan is more a "romantic occasion" than a religious holiday. "Boutique hotels" and "love hotels" have a field day. (日本のイブはどちらかと言うと恋愛のためのイベント。ブティックホテルやラブホテルが大繁盛する)

Japanese Culture 文化

Japanese Calendar

New Year's Shrine/Temple Visit
初詣
hatsu-moode

Coming-Of-Age Day
成人の日
(2nd Monday in Jan.)
seejin no hi

Bean-Throwing Ceremony
(to drive out bad luck)
節分
(Feb. 3)
setsubun

New Year's money gift for kids
お年玉
otoshidama

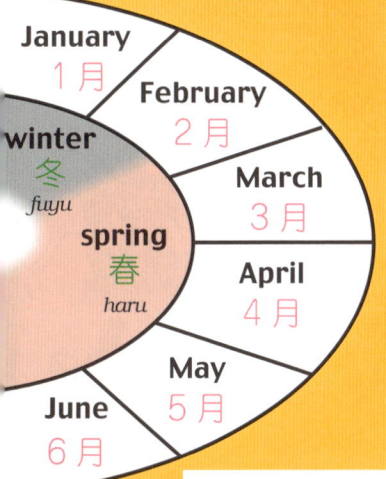

St. Valentine's Day
バレンタインデー
(Feb. 14)
barentain dee

Blossom-Viewing Season
花見
(March - April)
hanami

graduation
卒業式
(late March)
sotsugyoo-shiki

school entrance ceremony
入学式
(early April)
nyuugaku-shiki

- January 1月
- February 2月
- March 3月
- April 4月
- May 5月
- June 6月

winter 冬 fuyu
spring 春 haru

young graduates join work force
新入社員
(early April)
shin'nyuu shain

weather
天気
tenki

sunny
晴れ
hare

cloudy
くもり
kumori

rainy season **
梅雨
(early June - late July)
tsuyu

"Golden Week" holidays
ゴールデンウィーク
(last week of April to 1st week of May)
gooruden u'iiku

rainy 雨 ame
snowy 雪 yuki
windy 風が強い kaze ga tsuyo'i

** The end of the rainy season is marked by thunder, cumulonimbus and this author's birthday. From then on it's hot and humid as hell!（梅雨の終わりには雷と入道雲、さらには著者の誕生日がやってきて、その後はただもう死ぬほど蒸し暑くなる）

47

Japanese Culture 日本の文化 *nihon no bunka*

I am interested (in~). 興味があります *kyoomi ga arimas*	**traditional Japan** 伝統的な日本 *dentoo-teki-na nihon*
	**contemporary Japan** 今の日本 *ima no nihon*

日本の文化

Sumo wrestling 相撲 *sumoo*

Karate 空手 *karate*

Kendo 剣道 *kendoo*

Judo 柔道 *juudoo*

Noh theater 能 *noo*

Kabuki theater 歌舞伎 *kabuki*

miniaturized trees in pot 盆栽 *bonsai*

traditional puppet drama 人形浄瑠璃 *ningyoo jooruri*

traditional Japanese "banjo" *(technically classified as a type of lute)* 三味線 *shamisen*

traditional Japanese "horizontal harp" * *(technically classified as a type of zither)* 琴 *koto*

traditional "Kimono" clothes 着物 *kimono*

Japanese Dance 日本舞踊 *nihon-buyoo*

Japanese flower arrangement 生け花 *ikebana*

tea ceremony 茶道 *sadoo*

* The "koto" is sometimes known as Japan's national instrument, but the average Japanese only hears it played on New Year's Day variety shows on TV. (琴は日本を代表する楽器だが、日本人が音色を聞くのはTVの正月特番の時くらいなのだ…)

Japanese Culture 文化

still popular	new trend	now a fixture	thing of the past
今でも人気	新しいトレンド	すでに定着	過去の物
ima demo ninki	atarashii torendo	sude ni teechaku	kako no mono

cartoons
アニメ
anime

comic books
マンガ
manga

"Purikura" personalized stickers
プリクラ
puri-kura

"V" sign for the camera
Vサイン
bui-sain

smartphone overuse/addiction
スマホ依存
sumaho izon

rediscovery and appreciation of traditional Japan
日本らしさへの回帰
nihon rashisa e no kaiki

Japanese English
日本人英語
nihon-jin eego

mascot character craze
キャラクターブーム
kyarakutaa buumu

(quest for) self-improvement
自分磨き
jibun migaki

** Cool Japan
クールジャパン
kuuru japan

desire for stress relief
癒しを求める
iyashi o motomeru

diverse subcultures
多様なサブカルチャー
tayoo-na sabu karuchaa

feminized men and "stronger" women
男女の中性化
dan-jo no chuusee-ka

"otaku" culture
オタク文化
otaku bunka

** Some people think it is uncool to get excited about the government-led Cool Japan campaign. Ask your Japanese friends what they think.(国によるクールジャパン政策なんて…との意見もある。あなたの日本人の友達の意見は？)

Domestic Life in Japan 日本の家
nihon no i'e

Do you have it at home? あなたの家にありますか？ *anata no i'e ni arimas-ka*	I have it. あります *arimas*	I don't have it. ありません *arimasen*

1. air conditioner エアコン *e'akon*	2. flat panel television 薄型テレビ *usu-gata terebi*	3. (personal) computer パソコン *paso-con*	4. canned "shochu" cocktail 缶チューハイ *kan chuu-hai*
5. smartphone スマートフォン *sumaat-fon*	6. tatami mat 畳 *tatami*	7. comic books マンガ *manga*	8. electric mosquito repellent 電気蚊取り *denki ka-tori*

(50) Japanese apartments are quite small but many are given the ironic-sounding English label "mansion." （日本のアパートは狭いが、皮肉なことに「マンション：英語での意味は大邸宅」などという名前がついているものも多い）

Japanese Culture 文化

Domestic Life in Japan

1. fluorescent lamp 蛍光灯 *keekoo-too*	2. Buddhist altar 仏壇 *butsudan*	3. sliding paper door ふすま *fusuma*	4. futon mattress 布団 *futon*
5. short "hanten" coat はんてん *hanten*	6. hot sake 熱燗 *atsu-kan*	7. Japanese-style soup in a pot 鍋物 *nabemono*	8. portable gas cooker カセットコンロ *kasetto konro*
9. electric foot warmer こたつ *kotatsu*	10. handheld game player 携帯ゲーム *keetai geemu*	11. Japanese-style cushion 座布団 *zabuton*	**What's this?** これは何ですか？ *kore wa nan des-ka*

When something catches your eye, ask around. Be curious, but don't be too inquisitive. Some Japanese people get easily embarrassed. (興味をそそられたら質問を。ただ、あまり細々と聞くと、気恥ずかしがる人もいるので注意)

Major Sports in Japan
人気スポーツ *ninki-supootsu*

Which ~ do you like? 好きな～は？ *sukina ~ wa*	sport スポーツ *supootsu*	team チーム *chiimu*	player 選手 *senshu*
professional baseball プロ野球 *puro yakyuu*	Yomiuri Giants 巨人 *kyojin*	Tokyo Yakult Swallows ヤクルト *yakuruto*	Yokohama DeNA Bay Stars 横浜DeNA *yokohama*
Central League セリーグ *se-riigu*	Chunichi Dragons 中日 *chuunichi*	Hanshin Tigers 阪神 *hanshin*	Hiroshima Toyo Carp 広島 *hiroshima*
Pacific League パリーグ *pa-riigu*	*Hokkaido Nippon Ham Fighters 日本ハム *nippon hamu*	Tohoku Rakuten Golden Eagles 楽天 *rakuten*	Chiba Lotte Marines ロッテ *rotte*
home (stadium) 本拠地 *honkyochi* →P.18	Saitama Seibu Lions 西武 *seebu*	Orix Buffaloes オリックス *orikkusu*	Fukuoka Soft Bank Hawks ソフトバンク *sofuto banku*
Major League Baseball メジャーリーグ *mejaa riigu*	doing great 活躍してる *katsuyaku shiteru*	not doing very well あまり活躍してない *amari katsuyaku shite-nai*	traded トレードされた *toreedo sareta*
Japanese player 日本人選手 *nihon-jin senshu*	fan favorite 人気者 *ninki-mono*	sent down to the minors マイナー落ち *mainaa ochi*	retired 引退した *intai shita*
watching on TV テレビ観戦 *terebi kansen*	What time does it start? 何時から？ *nan-ji kara*	Which channel? 何チャンネル？ *nan-chan'neru*	Record it for me, please. 録画して下さい *rokuga-shite kudasai*

* Quite a few English-speakers become Fighters fans because they think the team is the Nippon "Ham Fighters." Why would you fight a ham, anyway? (英語圏の人は日本ハムがお好き。「ハムと戦う男たち」だと思って大ウケし、そのままファンになるようだ)

Japanese Culture 文化

professional soccer/football プロサッカー *puro sakkaa*	**J League** Jリーグ *jee riigu*	**J1/J2** J1/J2 *jee wan /jee tsuu*	**promotion/ demotion** 昇格／降格 *shookaku / kookaku*
World Cup ワールドカップ *waarudo kappu*	**Japanese national team** 日本代表チーム *nihon daihyoo chiimu*	**European football** 欧州サッカー *ooshuu sakkaa*	**changing clubs** 移籍 *iseki*
Sumo Wrestling 大相撲 *oozumoo*	** **Sumo Grand Champion** 横綱 *yokozuna*	**Sumo Junior Grand Champion** 大関 *oozeki*	**Sumo Champion** 関脇 *sekiwake*
Sumo Junior Champion 小結 *komusubi*	**Top Division Sumo Wrestler** 前頭 *ma'egashira*	**Second Division Sumo Wrestler** 十両 *juuryoo*	**sumo wrestler's stew** ちゃんこ *chanko*
sumo wrestler 力士 *rikishi*	**Japanese sumo wrestler** 日本人力士 *nihon-jin rikishi*	**non-Japanese sumo wrestler** 外国人力士 *gaikoku-jin rikishi*	**Mongolian sumo wrestler** モンゴル人力士 *mongoru-jin rikishi*
Who is your favorite? 誰のファン？ *dare no fan*	**swimming** 水泳 *sui'ee*	**golf** ゴルフ *gorufu*	**table tennis** 卓球 *takkyuu*
judo 柔道 *juudoo*	**figure skating** フィギュアスケート *figyua sukeeto*	**tennis** テニス *tenisu*	**martial arts** 格闘技 *kakutoogi*

Major Sports in Japan

Get a ticket for me (please). チケットを取って（下さい） *chiketto o totte (kudasai)*	**price** 値段 *nedan*	**place** 場所 *basho*	**time** 時間 *jikan*

** The Sumo Kyokai website sometimes changes sumo-related translations. To the dismay of non-Japanese speakers they now use many Japanese "romaji" descriptions. （相撲協会のHPは相撲用語の英訳が変わることもあり、現在は日本語のローマ字読みを多用中）

Well-known Japanese Food
有名な日本食
yuumee-na nihon-shoku

| I want to try/eat. 食べたい *tabe-tai* | Which restaurant do you recommend? どの店がいい（ですか）？ *dono mise ga ii (des-ka)* |

有名な日本食

Sukiyaki
すき焼き 
beef and vegetables cooked in sweetened soy sauce

Tempura
天ぷら 
deep-fried, battered seafood and vegetables

Sushi
寿司 
raw or cooked seafood on rolls of cooked rice

Tofu Ryoori
豆腐料理 
tofu dishes

Sashimi
刺身 
fresh slices of raw fish

Unagi no kaba-yaki *
うなぎの蒲焼 
eel steak grilled with sweetened soy sauce

Oden
おでん 
Japanese-style hotchpotch

Yakitori
焼鳥 
grilled chicken (and oft. vegetables) on sticks

Shabu Shabu
しゃぶしゃぶ 
slices of beef quickly cooked in hot, clear broth

Okonomi-yaki
お好み焼き 
Japanese-style hotplate pizza/pancake

| best/ fantastic 最高 *saikoo* | tasty/ delicious おいしい *oishii* | not bad なかなか *naka-naka* | different 珍しい *mezura shii* | not for me 苦手 *nigate* |

54 * Eels may remind you of snakes, but in Japan they are considered a delicacy that gives you an energy boost during the hot, humid summer.（外国人は姿がヘビのようだとして敬遠するウナギだが、日本では夏のスタミナ食である）

Enjoying Meals 1　食事 1

Ayu no shio-yaki
鮎の塩焼き 
grilled, salted sweetfish

Aji no tataki
アジのたたき 
finely chopped horse mackerel sashimi

Chawan-mushi
茶碗蒸し
egg custard steamed in a Japanese teacup

Teppan-yaki
鉄板焼き 
meat, seafood and vegetables grilled on a hotplate

Katsu-don
カツ丼 
rice topped with pork cutlet (oft. cooked)

Gyuu-don
牛丼 
rice topped with sweet, simmered beef and onion

Ten-don
天丼 
rice topped with tempura

Oyako-don
親子丼 
rice topped with chicken and egg

Kaisen-don
海鮮丼 
rice topped with assorted sashimi

Una-don
うな丼 
rice topped with grilled eel steak

Well-known Japanese Food

kind(s) →
種類
shurui

Kake
かけ
plain noodles in broth

Kitsune
きつね 
with fried bean curd

Tempura
天ぷら 
with tempura (oft. shrimp)

Soba
そば
buckwheat noodles (usu. thin)

Hiyashi
冷やし
served chilled

Tanuki
たぬき 
with tempura crusts

Tsukimi
月見 
with raw egg

Udon
うどん
white wheat noodles (usu. thick)

Zaru
ざる 
served cold with seaweed and dipping sauce

Karee Namban
カレー南蛮 
with curry sauce

Chikara
ちから 
with rice cake

Thank you. Let's eat. **
いただきます
itadaki-mas

Thank you for the meal.
ごちそうさま
gochisoo-sama

Check, please.
お勘定
okan'joo

＊＊ "Itadaki-mas" is said at the beginning of the meal to thank the cook and host. Unlike grace, this has no religious significance. (「いただきます」は食事の前の神への祈りではなく、食事を用意してくれた人への感謝の言葉)

55

Popular Home Cooking 家庭料理 *katee-ryoori*

homemade dish 家庭料理 *katee ryoori*	I like 好き *suki*	not for me 苦手 *nigate*	first time 初めて *hajimete*

家庭料理

Gohan ごはん — cooked/steamed rice

Miso-shiru 味噌汁 — miso soup

Furi-kake ふりかけ — flaky flavorings for cooked rice

Ocha-zuke お茶漬け — rice and toppings in tea (or broth)

Tamago-kake gohan* 卵かけごはん — rice mixed with raw egg and soy sauce

Tsukemono 漬物 — Japanese-style pickles

Ume-boshi 梅干し — pickled Japanese apricots

Nattoo 納豆 — fermented soybeans

Tamago-yaki 玉子焼き — Japanese-style omelet

Hiya-yakko 冷奴 — tofu served chilled with garnish

Niku-jaga 肉じゃが — stewed pork (or beef) and potatoes

Kimpira-goboo きんぴらごぼう — pan-fried burdock and carrot

Yaki-zakana 焼き魚 — grilled fish (oft. with the head and tail)

Nimono 煮物 — simmered vegetables and fish (or meat)

Nabe mono 鍋物 — Japanese-style soup/stew cooked in a large pot

---

56 * Fresh eggs are occasionally eaten raw in Japan. It is not a practical joke if you get a raw egg for your breakfast. (日本では新鮮な卵は生で食べることがある。朝食のごはんに生卵がついていたとしても、イタズラではないからね)

Enjoying Meals 1 食事 1

meal ごはん *gohan*

breakfast 朝食 *chooshoku*

lunch 昼食 *chuushoku*

dinner 夕食 *yuushoku*

set menu 定食 *teeshoku*

Japanese cuisine 和食 *washoku*

Western cuisine (oft. rather Japanized) 洋食 *yooshoku*

Popular Home Cooking

Yasai-itame 野菜炒め — *stir-fried vegetables*

Niku-itame 肉炒め — *stir-fried slices of beef/pork*

Tori no kara'age 鶏の唐揚げ — *deep-fried (boneless) chicken*

Ton-katsu トンカツ — *Japanese-style pork cutlet*

Ebi-furai エビフライ — *deep-fried, breaded prawns*

Omu-raisu オムライス — *fried, seasoned rice in omelet*

Suteeki ステーキ — *steak*

Supagetti スパゲティ — *spaghetti*

Guratan グラタン — *au gratin*

Karee Raisu カレーライス — *(Japanese-style) curry and rice*

Katsu Karee カツカレー — *curry and rice with pork cutlet*

Hayashi Raisu ハヤシライス — *rice with hashed beef*

** Hambaagu ハンバーグ — *hamburger steak*

Shichuu シチュー — *stew*

Yaki-niku 焼肉 — *Korean or Japanese-style barbecued meat*

** Notice the difference between "hambaagu" and "hambaagaa (P.59)." "Good" Japanese English has its semantics. Interesting, isn't it?（英語ではハンバーグもハンバーガーも同じ言葉。「正しい日本人英語」ではなぜか書き分ける。面白いでしょ）

Japanese Fast Food
日本のファーストフード *nihon no faasuto-fuudo*

Where can I buy?
どこで買えますか？
doko de ka'emas-ka

What do you recommend?
おすすめは？
osusume wa

Makuno-uchi Bentoo 幕の内弁当* — boxed meal with Japanese side dishes	**Chuuka Bentoo** 中華弁当 — boxed meal with Chinese side dishes	**Tori-no-kara'age bentoo** 鶏の唐揚げ弁当 — boxed meal with fried chicken
Shoga-yaki Bentoo 生姜焼き弁当 — boxed meal with ginger pork	**Hambaagu Bentoo** ハンバーグ弁当 — boxed meal with hamburger steak	**Ton-katsu Bentoo** トンカツ弁当 — boxed meal with pork cutlet

日本のファーストフード

Onigiri おにぎり — rice ball	**sake** 鮭 — salmon (usu. salted and grilled)	**okaka** おかか — bonito flakes with soy sauce	**ume-boshi** 梅干し — pickled Japanese apricot
tsuna ツナ — oiled, seasoned tuna flakes	**ikura** イクラ — seasoned salmon eggs	**mentaiko** 明太子 — pollack roe with red pepper sauce	**Yaki-onigiri** 焼きおにぎり — grilled rice ball (with soy sauce)

Kashi-pan 菓子パン — Japanese pastry with sweet filling	**An-pan** あんパン — bun with sweet bean filling	**Meron-pan** メロンパン — melon-flavored bun	**Karee-pan** カレーパン — fried bun with curry filling

sweet 甘い *amai*	**hot/spicy** 辛い *karai*	**sour** 酸っぱい *suppai*	**salty** しょっぱい *shoppai*	**bitter** 苦い *nigai*

* "Bento" is normally translated as "boxed lunch," but Japanese people eat "bento" all day. Convenience stores sell them 24 hours a day. (弁当はボックス・ランチという言葉で訳されるが、日本人は昼に限らずいつでも弁当を食べる)

Enjoying Meals 1 食事 1

Chinese cuisine 中華料理 *chuuka ryoori*

- **Gyooza** 餃子 — minced pork dumplings (oft. fried)
- **chuuka-don** 中華丼 — soupy stir-fry and rice
- **Chaahan** チャーハン — Chinese-style fried rice
- **Shuumai** シューマイ — pork (or seafood) dumplings (usu. steamed)
- **Hiyashi-chuuka** 冷やし中華 — chilled Chinese noodles with ham and vegetables
- **Harumaki** 春巻 — spring rolls
- **Maaboo-doofu** 麻婆豆腐 — tofu in spicy Chinese sauce
- **Yakisoba** 焼きそば — fried Chinese noodles

** Raamen ラーメン — Chinese-style noodles

- **aji** 味 — flavor of broth
- **oomori** 大盛り — large serving
- **chaashuu** チャーシュー — pork cooked in soy sauce and sake
- **shooyu** しょう油 — soy sauce
- **miso** 味噌 — salty soybean paste
- **Ton-kotsu** とんこつ — white pork broth
- **shio** 塩 — salt

Japanese Fast Food

- **hamburger** ハンバーガー — *hambaagaa*
- **French fries** (フライド)ポテト — *(furaido) poteto*
- **fried chicken** フライドチキン — *furaido chikin*
- **pizza** ピザ — *pizza*
- **sandwich** サンドイッチ — *sando-icchi*

Which restaurant do you recommend?
どこがおすすめ？
doko ga osusume?

What's the price range?
予算は？
yosan wa

- **French cuisine** フランス料理 — *furansu ryoori*
- **Thai cuisine** タイ料理 — *tai ryoori*
- **Indian cuisine** インド料理 — *indo ryoori*
- **Italian cuisine** イタリア料理 — *itaria ryoori*
- **Taiwanese cuisine** 台湾料理 — *taiwan ryoori*
- **Korean cuisine** 韓国料理 — *kankoku ryoori*

** "Raamen" has become more a gourmet food than a fast food. Lately fish stock (sakana no dashi) has become a popular "raamen" broth. Try it, it's delicious. (ラーメンはもはやグルメ食。最近のトレンドは魚のダシを使ったスープだ。うまいよ)

Japanese Sweets & Snacks
日本のおやつ *nihon no oyatsu*

| Japanese sweets 和菓子 *wagashi* | tea (tea break) お茶 *ocha* | break/rest ひと休み *hito-yasumi* |

Tai-yaki たい焼き
bream-shaped pancake 

Imagawa-yaki 今川焼き 
round pancake with sweet filling

Dora-yaki どら焼き 
sweat bean paste in browned sponge cake

*****Manjuu** まんじゅう 
sweet bean paste bun

Dango 団子 
rice dumplings with sweet or savory topping

Karintoo かりんとう 
deep-fried, sugar-coated dough

Daifuku 大福 
rice cake with sweet bean filling

Yookan ようかん 
chunky sweet bean jelly

Ohagi おはぎ 
rice ball with sweet bean coating

Sembee せんべい 
Japanese rice crackers

Okaki おかき 
grilled or fried slices of rice cake

Mame-gashi 豆菓子 
snack food with beans or nuts

Uji Kintoki 宇治金時 
shaved ice with sweet bean paste & green tea syrup

Monaka 最中 
sweet bean paste in wafers

Kuriimu An'Mitsu クリームあんみつ 
parfait with bean paste and ice cream

Tokoro-ten ところてん 
seaweed gelatin strips in tangy broth

Abekawa mochi 安倍川餅 
rice cake in sweet bean powder

Isobe-maki 磯辺巻き 
savory rice cake in "nori" seaweed

(60) * Also remember to try "an'man." It resembles a white "manju," but is much larger and served steaming hot in autumn and winter. (あんまんも食べてみよう。白いまんじゅうを大きくしたようなあんまんは、寒い季節にホカホカのを味わおう)

Enjoying Meals 1 食事 1

I'm hungry お腹すいた *onaka suita*	snack / refreshments おやつ *oyatsu*	midnight snack 夜食 *yashoku*
What's popular? 何が人気（ですか）？ *nani ga ninki (des-ka)* **	snack food スナック *sunakku*	ice cream アイス *aisu*
sweets / snack food お菓子 *okashi*	Japanese sweets 和菓子 *wagashi*	Western-style sweets 洋菓子 *yoogashi*

Japanese Sweets & Snacks

Kappa Ebi-sen かっぱえびせん *roasted, shrimp-flavor wheat sticks*	**Jagariko** じゃがりこ *deep-fried, steamed potato sticks*	**Chiizu Aamondo** チーズアーモンド *rice cracker with cheese & almond*
Koara no Maachi コアラのマーチ *koala biscuits with sweet filling*	**Kaki-no-Tane** 柿の種 *tiny rice crackers (oft. with peanuts)*	**Burakku Sandaa** ブラックサンダー *chocolate bar with cookie bits*
Bebii Staa Raamen ベビースターラーメン *deep-fried noodle bits*	**Kyarameru Koon** キャラメルコーン *caramel-coated corn puffs*	**Ottotto** おっとっと *tiny fish-shaped potato crackers*
Pokkii ポッキー *chocolate-coated biscuit sticks*	**Happii Taan** ハッピーターン *rice crackers with sweet & salty seasoning*	**Umai-Boo** うまい棒 *savory corn puff stick*
Tako-yaki たこ焼き *fried octopus dumplings*	**Monja-yaki** もんじゃ焼き *fried flour porridge (with ingredients of your choice)*	* **Chuuka-Man** 中華まん *steamed Chinese-style stuffed bun*

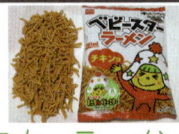

** New "sunakku" foods come and go, but these are the all-time favorites which have survived the test of time and are still going strong. (新しいスナックが出ては消えゆく中、ここに取り上げたのは時代を超えて食べつがれる歴戦の猛者である)

Vegetables & Fruits 野菜と果物 *yasai to kudamono*

How much is one of these? ひとついくら？ *hitotsu ikura*	How much for a package? ひとパックいくら？ *hito-pakku ikura*	How much for 100 grams? 100グラムいくら？ *hyaku-guramu ikura*

vegetables 野菜 *yasai*	potato じゃがいも *jaga-imo*	sweet potato さつまいも *satsuma-imo*	kidney beans いんげん *ingen*	burdock ごぼう *goboo*
green onion 長ネギ *naga-negi*	onion タマネギ *tama-negi*	spinach ほうれん草 *hoorensoo*	garlic ニンニク *nin'niku*	carrot にんじん *ninjin*
Chinese cabbage 白菜 *hakusai*	cabbage キャベツ *kyabetsu*	lettuce レタス *retasu*	bamboo sprout たけのこ *takenoko*	eggplant ナス *nasu*
"daikon" radish 大根 *daikon*	lotus root 蓮根 *renkon*	*"shiitake" mushroom しいたけ *shiitake*	"shimeji" mushroom しめじ *shimeji*	red pepper とうがらし *toogarashi*
green soybeans 枝豆 *eda-mame*	garlic chive ニラ *nira*	cucumber きゅうり *kyuuri*	green pepper ピーマン *piiman*	bean sprouts もやし *moyashi*
fruits 果物 *kudamono*	grapes ぶどう *budoo*	persimmon かき *kaki*	peach もも *momo*	strawberry いちご *ichigo*
loquat/Japanese medlar びわ *biwa*	melon メロン *meron*	tangerine みかん *mikan*	*"summer" orange 夏みかん *natsu-mikan*	grapefruit グレープフルーツ *gureepu-furuutsu*
apple りんご *ringo*	cherry さくらんぼ *sakurambo*	pineapple パイナップル *pai'nappuru*	watermelon すいか *suika*	pear なし *nashi*

野菜と果物

* Some vegetables and fruits don't have "correct" English names. Try to say their Japanese names and you'll be sure to impress "the locals." (英訳しづらい野菜や果物名を日本語で言えると、日本人から尊敬の目で見られる)

Enjoying Meals 2　食事２

English	Japanese	Romaji
rice	米	kome
rice cake	餅	mochi
buckwheat noodles	そば	soba
white wheat noodles	うどん	udon
tofu / bean curd	豆腐	toofu
fried bean curd	油揚げ	abura-age
fried bean curd mixed with vegetables	がんもどき	gam'modoki
devil's tongue jelly *	こんにゃく	kon'nyaku
fermented soybeans	納豆	nattoo
bread	パン	pan
loaf of white bread	食パン	shoku-pan
butter	バター	bataa
margarine	マーガリン	maagarin
jam	ジャム	jamu
instant noodles in a cup	カップ麺	kappu men
canned food	缶詰	kanzume
frozen food	冷凍食品	reetoo shokuhin
"boil-in-the-bag" food	レトルト食品	retoruto shokuhin
baby food	ベビーフード	bebii fuudo
mayonnaise	マヨネーズ	mayo-neezu
dressing	ドレッシング	dores-shingu
Chinese-style spicy oil	ラー油	raayu
sauce	ソース	soosu
pepper	コショー	koshoo
salt	塩	shi'o
sugar	砂糖	satoo
miso / soybean paste **	味噌	miso
soy sauce	醤油	shooyu
"mirin" sweet cooking liquor	みりん	mirin
vinegar	酢	su
grated red pepper	一味	ichi-mi
7-flavor red pepper mix	七味	shichi-mi
Japanese horseradish	わさび	wasabi
mustard	からし	karashi
cooking knife	包丁	hoochoo
cutting board	まな板	mana'ita
dishcloth	布巾	fukin
plate	皿	sara
chopsticks	箸	hashi
rice bowl	茶碗	chawan
teacup	湯のみ茶碗	yunomi jawan
soup bowl	お椀	o-wan
teapot	急須	kyuusu
cooking pot	鍋	nabe

Vegetables & Fruits

** Watch out for "miso." It looks like peanut butter, but don't spread it over your bread. If you do, you're in for a salty shock. Don't say I didn't warn you!（味噌をピーナツバターと間違えてパンに塗らないように。しょっぱいぞ！）

Seafood & Meat 魚と肉 *sakana to niku*

fish 魚 *sakana*	**Pacific saury** サンマ *sam'ma*	**sardine** イワシ *iwashi*	**Akta mackerel** ホッケ *hokke*	**horse mackerel** アジ *aji*
"shishamo" smelt シシャモ *shishamo*	**herring** ニシン *nishin*	**mackerel** サバ *saba*	**yellowtail** ブリ *buri*	**young yellowtail** ハマチ *hamachi*
salmon 鮭 *sake*	**tuna** マグロ *maguro*	**amberjack** カンパチ *kampachi*	**bonito** カツオ *katsuo*	**sea bream** タイ *tai*
whiting キス *kisu*	**"karee" flatfish** カレイ *karee*	**"hirame" flatfish** ヒラメ* *hirame*	**cod** タラ *tara*	**cutlass fish** タチウオ *tachi-u'o*
eel ウナギ *unagi*	**conger eel** 穴子 *anago*	**octopus** タコ *tako*	**squid** イカ *ika*	**sea urchin** ウニ *uni*
shrimp / prawn エビ *ebi*	**Japanese spiny lobster** 伊勢エビ *ise-ebi*	**"sweet" shrimp** 甘エビ *ama-ebi*	**horse-hair crab** 毛ガニ *ke-gani*	**king crab** タラバガニ *taraba-gani*
oyster 牡蠣 *kaki*	**clam** ハマグリ *hamaguri*	**short-necked clam** アサリ *asari*	**fresh water clam** シジミ *shijimi*	**topshell** サザエ *saza'e*
sweetfish アユ *ayu*	**rainbow trout** ニジマス *niji-masu*	**pond smelt** ワカサギ *wakasagi*	**carp** コイ *koi*	**What's this?** これ、何？ *kore, nani*

魚と肉

* The way Japanese tell flatfish apart is interesting. Those with eyes on the left are called "Hirame" and those with eyes on the right are called "Karee." (日本では目の位置でヒラメとカレイを判別する。「左ヒラメに右カレイ」なのである)

Enjoying Meals 2 　食事2

how to cook　料理の仕方　ryoori no shikata

English	Japanese	Romaji
grill	焼く	yaku
stew	煮る	niru
eat without (additional) cooking	そのまま食べる	sonomama taberu
steam	蒸す	musu
stir-fry	炒める	itameru
(deep-)fry	揚げる	ageru
boil	ゆでる	yuderu
dried/sun-dried	干物	himono
raw/uncooked	生	nama
lightly salted	ひと塩	hito-shi'o
flavored	味つき	aji-tsuki
in season	旬	shun
salted pollack roe	タラコ	tarako
*salmon roe	筋子	sujiko
*salmon eggs	イクラ	ikura
tube-shaped fish cake	竹輪	chikuwa
fish paste cake	かまぼこ	kamaboko
fish and yam patty	はんぺん	hampen
"wakame" seaweed	ワカメ	wakame
"kombu" kelp	昆布	kombu
"nori" seaweed	のり	nori
dried bonito (flakes)	かつお節	katsuo-bushi
beef	牛肉	gyuu-niku
pork	豚肉	buta-niku
chicken	鶏肉	tori-niku
ham	ハム	hamu
bacon	ベーコン	beekon
spaghetti	スパゲティ	supagetti
Chinese(-style) noodles	ラーメン	raamen
egg	卵	tamago
cheese	チーズ	chiizu
Japanese deli food	惣菜	soozai
fried potato dumpling	コロッケ	korokke
cutlet	カツ	katsu
fried cake of minced meat	メンチカツ	menchi-katsu
fried food	フライ	furai

Seafood & Meat

* "Sujiko" is usually redder and more salty. "Ikura" is only lightly salted and is regarded as the gourmet's choice. （筋子とイクラはどちらも鮭の卵。筋子は赤っぽく塩辛いが、イクラはひと塩でよりグルメ度が高いとされている）

Beverages 飲み物 *nomimono*

 **I am thirsty.** 喉が渇いた *nodo ga kawaita*	**I want to drink.** 飲みたい *nomi-tai*	**Please (give me).** 下さい *kudasai*
beverage 飲み物 *nomimono* 	**water** 水 *mizu* 	**mineral water** ミネラルウォーター *mineraru wootaa*
Japanese tea  お茶 *ocha*	**green tea** 緑茶 *ryoku-cha*	**"sencha" tea** 煎茶 *sen-cha* (early-season "medium-grade" tea)	**"bancha" tea** 番茶 *ban-cha* (late-season "coarse" tea)
powdered green tea  抹茶 *maccha*	**green tea with brown rice flavor** 玄米茶 *gem'mai-cha*	**barley tea** 麦茶 *mugi-cha* 	**savory kelp tea** こぶ茶 *kobu-cha*
 **coffee** コーヒー *koohii*	**"American-style" weak coffee** アメリカン *amerikan*	**blended coffee** ブレンド *burendo*	**cold/hot** アイス / ホット *aisu/hotto*
tea (English-style)  紅茶 *koocha*	**lemon** レモン *remon* 	**sugar** 砂糖 *satoo* 	**cream/milk** ミルク *miruku* 
hot chocolate/cocoa  ココア *coco'a*	 **milk** 牛乳 *gyuu-nyuu*	**soybean milk**  豆乳 *too-nyuu*	**oolong tea** 烏龍茶 *uuron-cha*
 **soft drink** ジュース *juusu*	*** juice**  100%ジュース *hyaku paasento juusu*	**carbonated drink** 炭酸飲料 *tansan inryo*	**sports drink** スポーツドリンク *supootsu dorinku*

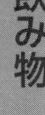

* In Japan, nearly all soft drinks are called "juusu / juice." You have to say "100% juusu" when you want bona fide fruit juice. (日本ではあらゆるソフトドリンクをジュースと呼ぶため、ハッキリと果汁100%と言わないと本物にありつけない)

Enjoying Meals 2 食事2

Where can I drink?
どこで飲めますか？
doko de nomemas-ka

Where can I buy?
どこで買えますか？
doko de ka'emas-ka

What do you recommend?
おすすめは？
osusume wa

liquor 酒 sake	Sake (Japanese rice wine) 日本酒 nihon-shu	sweet 甘口 ama-kuchi	dry 辛口 kara-kuchi
plum liqueur 梅酒 ume-shu	shao-hsing rice wine 紹興酒 shookoo-shu	"Shochu" spirits 焼酎 shoochuu	whiskey ウイスキー u'isukii
wine ワイン wain	red 赤 aka	white 白 shiro	rosé ロゼ roze
Shochu-based cocktail ** チューハイ chuu-hai	shochu cocktail with oolong tea ウーロンハイ uuron-hai	shochu cocktail with lemon レモンハイ remon-hai	with a pickled Japanese apricot 梅干し入り umeboshi-iri
beer ビール biiru	lager ラガー ragaa	draught/draft 生 nama	on tap 生 nama
dark/stout 黒 kuro	dry ドライ dorai	local beer 地ビール ji-biiru	low-malt beer-style liquor 発泡酒 happoo-shu

Suntory サントリー	Asahi アサヒ	Kirin キリン	Ebisu エビス	Sapporo サッポロ

Beverages

** Many "izaka-ya" bars have a large variety of "chuu-hai" cocktails. Check out their house specials and local specialties. （酎ハイの種類を豊富に取り揃えている居酒屋も多い。店のおすすめやご当地酎ハイは要チェック）

Going Out for a Drink
飲みに行く・カラオケ *nomi ni iku / karaoke*

* Let's go drinking. 飲みに行こう *nomi ni ikoo*	**Table for how many?** 何名様で？ *nan-mee-sama de*	**Three, (please).** 3人（です） *san nin (des)* → P.37
Japanese-style bar & grill 居酒屋 *izaka-ya*	**Yoro no Taki** 養老の滝 *yooroo no taki*	**Sho-ya** 庄や *shoo-ya*	**Shiraki-ya** 白木屋 *shiraki-ya*

Sake 日本酒 *nihon-shu*	**cold/hot** 冷/熱燗 *hiya/atsukan*	**Sake cup** おちょこ *ochoko*	**How many?** いくつ？ *ikutsu*
beer in a medium mug 中生 *chuu-nama*	**beer in a large mug** 大生 *dai-nama*	**bottled beer** 瓶ビール *bin-biiru*	**glass** グラス *gurasu*
whiskey ウイスキー *u'isukii*	**straight** ストレート *sutoreeto*	**on the rocks** ロック *rokku*	**with water** 水割り *mizu-wari*
			with soda ソーダ割り *sooda-wari*

飲みに行く・カラオケ

appetizer/sidedish つまみ *tsumami*	**Moro-kyuu** もろキュー *cucumber with miso paste*	**Ko-ebi no kara-age** 小エビの唐揚げ *deep-fried baby shrimp*	**Tori nankotsu-age** 鶏ナンコツ揚げ *fried chicken cartilage*
Koon bataa コーンバター *corn stir-fried in butter*	**Potato Furai** ポテトフライ *French-fried potatoes*	**Edamame** 枝豆 *boiled green soybeans*	**What do you recommend?** おすすめは？ *osusume wa*
Menu, please. メニュー、下さい *menyuu, kudasai*	**Chopsticks, please.** 箸、下さい *hashi, kudasai*	**Plate, please.** 取り皿下さい *torizara, kudasai*	**drunk/drunkard** 酔っ払い *yopparai*

* Drinking with Japanese is quite fun—if you don't mind personal questions, mutual pouring of drinks, and repeated offers of sake from everyone around you. (日本人と飲むのは楽しい ― 個人的な質問や「飲め飲め」とすすめられるのが平気なら…)

Enjoying Meals 2 食事２

Let's go and sing Karaoke.	karaoke box/parlor	Japanese "snack" bar
カラオケに行こう *kara'oke ni ikoo*	カラオケボックス *kara'oke bokkusu*	スナック *sunakku*

What's the charge/rate?	English songs available?	Teach me Japanese songs.
料金は？ *ryookin wa*	英語の歌、ある？ *eego no uta, aru*	日本の歌、教えて *nihon no uta, oshi'ete*

Raise the key. キーを上げて *kii o agete*	the best 最高 *saikoo*	quite good 上手 *joozu*	terrible 下手 *heta*
Lower the key. キーを下げて *kii o sagete*	fabulous すごい *sugoi*	doing okay まあまあ *maamaa*	tone-deaf 音痴 *onchi*

Japan's old-fashioned pop songs 演歌 *enka*	pop songs ポップス *poppusu*	Anime theme songs アニメソング *anime songu*	English songs 洋楽 *yoogaku*
What's the song called? 何て歌？ *nan-te uta*	Who sings it? 誰の歌？ *dare no uta*	I love this song. この歌、いいね *kono uta, iine*	I want to learn this song. この歌、覚えたい *kono uta, obo'e-tai*
Do you know this one? これ、知ってる？ *kore, shitteru*	I can sing this. これ、歌える *kore, uta'eru*	Who's your favorite singer? 好きな歌手は？ *suki-na kashu wa*	I want this song. この歌、欲しい *kono uta hoshii*

Check, please.	go Dutch	＊＊ to treat someone	hangover
お勘定 *okanjoo*	割り勘 *wari-kan*	おごり *ogori*	二日酔い *futsuka-yoi*

＊＊ Japanese love to treat their guests, but it's good manners for you to decline even if you have no money (and pray they will pick up the tab in the end). (お金がなくて奢りを期待してる時も「払います」と言うのがマナー……本当に奢ってもらえますように)

Going Out for a Drink

What Time? 時間と時計
jikan to tokee

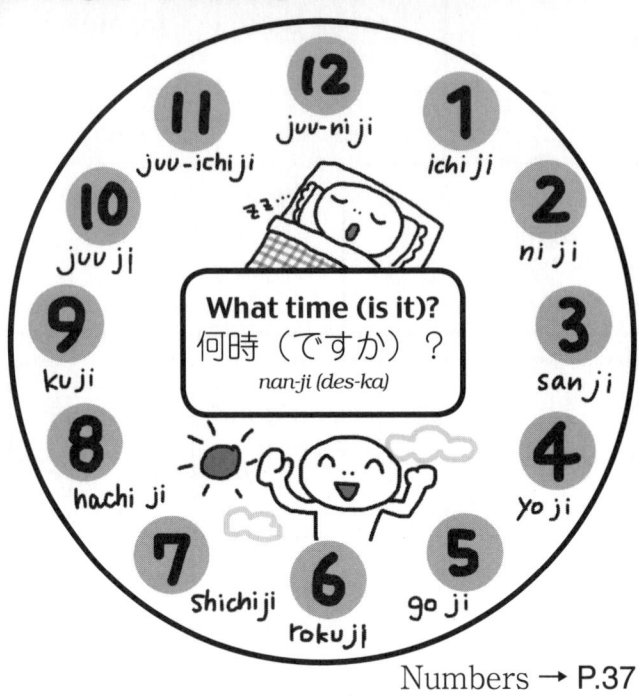

Clock

- 12 — juu-ni ji
- 1 — ichi ji
- 2 — ni ji
- 3 — san ji
- 4 — yo ji
- 5 — go ji
- 6 — roku ji
- 7 — shichi ji
- 8 — hachi ji
- 9 — ku ji
- 10 — juu ji
- 11 — juu-ichi ji

What time (is it)?
何時（ですか）？
nan-ji (des-ka)

Numbers → P.37

Times of Day

English	日本語	Romaji
morning	朝	asa
noon	正午	shoogo
afternoon	昼	hiru
evening	夕方	yuugata
night	夜	yoru
midnight	夜中	yonaka

Telling Time

It's 8 o'clock.	About eight.	five to eight	five past eight
8時です	8時頃です	8時5分前	8時5分（過ぎ）
hachi ji des	hachi ji goro des	hachi ji go fun ma'e	hachi ji go fun (sugi)

quarter past eight	half past eight	eight thirty	MEMO
8時15分	8時半	8時30分	
hachi ji juu-go fun	hachi ji han	hachi ji san-jippun (san-juppun)	

What's the time?	hour(s)	minute(s)	second(s)
何時何分？	時間	分	秒
nan-ji nam-pun	jikan	fun/pun	byoo

can make it	right on time	too early	I'll be late.
間に合う	時間ピッタリ	早すぎ	遅れます
mani'a'u	jikan pittari *	haya-sugi	okure-mas **

* Many Japanese have cutting-edge high-tech phones with clock/schedule functions to help them stay on schedule. Do they arrive on time? Well, not always ... （スケジュール機能付きの最先端のスマホがあっても、遅れる人は遅れてくるものだ）

When & What Time? 約束

| What time should we meet? 何時にする? *nan-ji ni suru* | Where should we meet? どこにする? *doko ni suru* | I can make it. 行けます *ikemas* | I can't make it. 無理です *muri des* |

(Please) come and pick me up.
迎えに来て（下さい）
muka'e ni kite (kudasai)

I will come and pick you up.
迎えに行きます
muka'e ni ikimas

Give me your cellphone number.
携帯、教えて
keetai, oshi'ete

I will call you.
電話します
den'wa shimas
→ P.82

Please call me.
電話下さい
den'wa kudasai

| What time is the bus? 何時のバス? *nan-ji no basu* | What time is the train? 何時の電車? *nan-ji no densha* | What time is the plane? 何時の飛行機? *nan-ji no hikooki* | What's the arrival time? 何時着? *nan-ji-chaku* |

How long does it take?
どの位かかりますか？
dono kurai kakarimas-ka

How many hours?
何時間くらい？
nan-jikan kurai

How many minutes?
何分くらい？
nam-pun kurai

What time does it begin?
何時から（ですか）？
nan-ji kara (des-ka)

What time does it end?
何時まで（ですか）？
nan-ji made (des-ka)

What Time?

| I'm sorry. ごめんなさい *gomen'nasai* | I made a mistake. 間違えました *machiga'e-mashita* | time 時間 *jikan* | place 場所 *basho* |

| I got too busy. 忙しくなりすぎてしまって *isogashiku nari-sugite shimatte* | I got lost. 迷いました *mayoi-mashita* | I lost the phone number. 電話番号をなくしました *den'wa bangoo o nakushi-mashita* |

** When you find yourself running late, email a message from your phone to that effect. In Japan it is bad manners to talk on the phone on trains and buses. (車内マナーもあるのでバスや電車からの遅れますメッセージはメールがおすすめ)

Days, Weeks & Months
月日と年月 tsuki-hi to nen-getsu

When?
いつ（ですか）？
itsu (des-ka)

yesterday 昨日 kinoo	**2 weeks ago** ２週間前 ni-shuu-kan ma'e	**Mon** 月曜日 getsu-yoobi
	last week 先週 sen-shuu	**Tue** 火曜日 ka-yoobi
		Wed 水曜日 sui-yoobi
	this week 今週 kon-shuu	**Thu** 木曜日 moku-yoobi
today 今日 kyoo	**next week** 来週 rai-shuu	**Fri** 金曜日 kin-yoobi
		Sat 土曜日 do-yoobi
tomorrow 明日 ashita	**in 3 weeks** ３週間後 san-shuu-kan go	**Sun** 日曜日 nichi-yoobi

月日と年月

3 months ago ３か月前 san-kagetsu ma'e	**last month** 先月 sen-getsu	**this month** 今月 kon-getsu	**next month** 来月 rai-getsu	**in 2 months** ２か月後 ni-kagetsu go
2 years ago ２年前 ni-nen ma'e	**last year** 去年 kyo-nen	**this year** 今年 kotoshi	**next year** 来年 rai-nen	**in 3 years** ３年後 san-nen go

＊ **In what year?** (of the Western calendar) （西暦）何年ですか？ (seereki) nan-nen des-ka	**Taisho** (1912~1926) 大正 taishoo	**Showa** (1926~1989) 昭和 shoowa	**Heisei** (1989~) 平成 heesee

＊ The Japanese calendar calculates the year from the first year of the emperor's reign. When a new emperor is enthroned, a new era begins—leading to considerable confusion! (新しい年号とは、世の中に混乱をもたらすものでもある)

When & What Time? 約束

Month	Japanese	Romaji
January	1月 / 一月	ichi-gatsu
February	2月 / 二月	ni-gatsu
March	3月 / 三月	san-gatsu
April	4月 / 四月	shi-gatsu
May	5月 / 五月	go-gatsu
June	6月 / 六月	roku-gatsu
July	7月 / 七月	shichi-gatsu
August	8月 / 八月	hachi-gatsu
September	9月 / 九月	ku-gatsu
October	10月 / 十月	juu-gatsu
November	11月 / 十一月	juu-ichi-gatsu
December	12月 / 十二月	juu-ni-gatsu

When can we meet? いつ会えますか？ *itsu a'emas-ka*

What is your schedule? 都合はどう（ですか）？ *tsugoo wa doo (des-ka)*

Please write it down. 書いて下さい *kaite kudasai*

What day of the week? 何曜日？ *nan-yoobi*

What day of the month? 何月何日？ *nan-gatsu nan-nichi*

What time? 何時？ *nan-ji* → P.70

Where? どこで？ *doko de*

weekday 平日 *hee-jitsu*

holiday/day-off 休日 *kyuu-jitsu*

public holiday 祝日 *shuku-jitsu*

weekend 週末 *shuu-matsu*

holidays in a row 連休 *ren-kyuu*

paid holiday 有休 *yuu-kyuu*

child-care leave 育児休暇 *ikuji kyuuka*

birthday 誕生日 *tanjoo-bi*

wedding anniversary 結婚記念日 *kekkon kinem-bi*

Chinese zodiac signs ** (for your "birth-year") 十二支 *juu-ni-shi*

What's your Chinese zodiac sign? 何年ですか？ *nani-doshi des-ka*

How old are you? おいくつ（ですか）？ *oikutsu (des-ka)*

Sign	Japanese	Romaji
Rat	ねずみ/子	nezumi
Ox	うし/丑	ushi
Tiger	とら/寅	tora
Rabbit	うさぎ/卯	usagi
Dragon	たつ/辰	tatsu
Serpent	へび/巳	hebi
Horse	うま/午	uma
Sheep	ひつじ/未	hitsuji
Monkey	さる/申	saru
Bird	とり/酉	tori
Dog	いぬ/戌	inu
Wild Boar	いのしし/亥	inoshishi

** Some old folks like the personality comparisons of Chinese zodiac signs, while younger Japanese tend to think your blood type has more to do with your personality. （世代が下の日本人ほど十二支より血液型のが気質に関係ありと見ているようだ）

Drugstores & Clinics 薬局・病院 *yakkyoku / byoo'in*

Where? どこ？ *doko*	drugstore 薬局 *yakkyoku*	hospital 病院 *byoo'in*

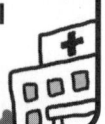

I want medicine (for ～). *薬が欲しい *kusuri ga hoshii*	headache 頭痛 *zutsuu*	stomachache 腹痛 *fukutsuu*	heartburn 胸焼け *mune-yake*
toothache 歯が痛い *ha ga itai*	nausea 吐き気 *hakike*	motion sickness 乗り物酔い *norimono-yoi*	anemia 貧血 *hinketsu*
runny nose 鼻水 *hana-mizu*	hay fever 花粉症 *kafun-shoo*	fever 熱 *netsu*	cold カゼ *kaze*
constipation 便秘 *bempi*	indigestion 消化不良 *shooka furyoo*	diarrh(o)ea 下痢 *geri*	cough せき *seki*
backache 腰痛 *yootsuu*	menstrual pain 生理痛 *seeri-tsuu*	insect bite 虫さされ *mushi-sasare*	itchness かゆみ *kayumi*
cut 切り傷 *kiri-kizu*	graze すり傷 *suri-kizu*	burn やけど *yakedo*	sunburn 日焼けの痛み *hiyake no itami*
stiff neck/shoulders 肩こり *kata-kori*	bruise 打ち身 *uchimi*	muscular pain 筋肉痛 *kin'niku-tsuu*	sprain 捻挫 *nenza*
fatigue 疲労 *hiroo*	eye fatigue 眼のつかれ *me no tsukare*	dizziness めまい *memai*	skin irritation 肌荒れ *hada-are*

* Japanese drugs are generally less potent than their Western equivalents. Ask your doctor or pharmacist about adjusting the dosage. (日本の薬は西洋の薬よりも弱め。多めに飲む必要がある時は、医者や薬剤師に相談しよう)

Emergencies トラブル

constant pain ずっと痛い *zutto itai*	**sharp pain** 鋭い痛み *surudoi itami*
sporadic pain 時々痛い *tokidoki itai*	**dull pain** 鈍い痛み *nibui itami*

I'm in pain.
痛い
itai

eye 目 *me*	**** head** 頭 *atama*	**ear** 耳 *mimi*	**nose** 鼻 *hana*
shoulder 肩 *kata*	**tooth/teeth** 歯 *ha*	**tongue** 舌 *shita*	**neck** 首 *kubi*
arm 腕 *ude*			**throat** 喉 *nodo*
breasts 胸 / 乳房 *mune / chibusa*			**chest** 胸 / 胸板 *mune / muna'ita*
elbow ひじ *hiji*			**back** 背中 *senaka*
rib あばら *abara*			**lower back** 腰 *koshi*
stomach おなか *onaka*			**wrist** 手首 *tekubi*
buttocks おしり *oshiri*			**hand** 手 *te*
anus 肛門 *koomon*			**finger** 指 *yubi*
thigh (太)もも *(futo-)momo*			**shin** すね *sune*
knee ひざ *hiza*			**leg** 脚 *ashi*
calf ふくらはぎ *fukurahagi*	**genitals** 性器 *seeki*		**ankle** 足首 *ashikubi*
toe つま先 *tsumasaki*	**vagina** 女性器 *joseeki*	**penis** 男性器 *danseeki*	**foot** 足 *ashi*

Drugstores & Clinics

** "Warui" is a handy phrase to describe the affected/painful part. But don't say "warui" for your head. "Atama (head) ga warui," means "I'm stupid." (不調な部分を表わす「悪い」という言葉だが、「頭」に関して使うと「バカ」という意味になるので注意)

At the Hospital
通院・入院
tsuu'in / nyuu'in

Take me to a hospital (please).
病院に連れてって（下さい）
byoo'in ni tsure-tette (kudasai)

Call an ambulance (please).
救急車を呼んで（下さい）
kyuukyuu-sha o yonde (kudasai)

internal medicine 内科 naika	surgery 外科 geka	orthopedics 整形外科 seekee-geka	dentistry 歯科 shika
obstetrics & gynecology 産婦人科 sanfujin-ka	pediatrics 小児科 shooni-ka	psychiatry 精神科 seeshin-ka	ENT specialist 耳鼻科 jibika
STD specialist 性病科 seebyoo-ka	urology 泌尿器科 hi'nyooki-ka	dermatology 皮膚科 hifu-ka	ophthalmology 眼科 ganka

Do you (they) understand English?
英語が通じますか？＊
eego ga tsuujimas-ka

Can I get on with my trip?
旅行を続けられますか？
ryokoo o tsuzuke-raremas-ka

How long do I need to recover?
どの位で治りますか？
dono-kurai de na'orimas-ka

body temperature 体温 tai'on	pulse 脈 myaku	urine 尿 nyoo	appetite 食欲 shoku-yoku
symptom 症状 shoojoo	bleeding 出血 shukketsu	allergy アレルギー arerugii	medical history 過去の病気 kako no byooki

通院・入院

血液型	**blood type**		気管支	**windpipe**
	ketsu'eki-gata			kikan-shi
動脈	**artery**		心臓	**heart**
	doo-myaku			shinzoo
静脈	**vein**		肺	**lungs**
	joo-myaku			hai
肝臓	**liver**		胃	**stomach**
	kanzoo			i
腎臓	**kidney**		脾臓	**spleen**
	jinzoo			hizoo
膀胱	**bladder**		大腸	**large intestine**
	bookoo			dai-choo
			小腸	**small intestine**
				shoo-choo

＊ Doctors know how to read and write in English, but not many of them are good English speakers. How about selling them a copy of my phrasebook? (英語の読み書きはできても会話は苦手な先生もいる。通院ついでにこの本をすすめといてね)

Emergencies トラブル

doctor 先生 sensee	**I have high blood pressure.** 高血圧です koo-ketsuatsu des	**I have low blood pressure.** 低血圧です tee-ketsuatsu des
nurse 看護師（さん） kango-shi (san)	**I'm having my period.** 生理中です seeri-chuu des	**I'm pregnant.** 妊娠中です ninshin-chuu des

examination 診察 shinsatsu	**treatment** 治療 chiryoo	**injection** 注射 chuusha	**diagnosis** 診断 shindan
X-ray レントゲン rentogen	**hospitalization** 入院 nyuu'in	**intravenous drip** 点滴 tenteki	**anesthetic** 麻酔 masui
operation 手術 shujutsu	**prescription** 処方箋 shohoo-sen	**pharmacy** 薬局 yakkyoku	**insurance** 保険 hoken

flu インフルエンザ infuru'enza	**hepatitis** 肝炎 kan-en	**neuralgia** 神経痛 shinkee-tsuu	**cystitis** 膀胱炎 bookoo-en
measles はしか hashika	**hives** じんましん jim'mashin	**food poisoning** 食中毒 shoku-chuudoku	**gastritis** 胃炎 i-en
neurosis ノイローゼ noirooze	**hernia** ヘルニア heruni'a	**fracture** 骨折 kossetsu	**whiplash** ムチ打ち muchi-uchi
stomach ulcer 胃潰瘍 i-kaiyoo	**hemorrhoids** 痔 ji	**appendicitis** 盲腸 moochoo	*** * STD** (sexually transmitted disease) 性病 see-byoo

At the Hospital

* * Some Japanese magazine articles say that these days it is "safer" to have your fun with "professionals" than with regular fun-seekers on the street. （シロートのほうが「プロ」よりも危険度が高い、なんていう雑誌の記事を見かけたりもする）

Emergencies トラブル *toraburu*

Help! 助けて（下さい）！ *tasukete (kudasai)*

Catch him/her! 捕まえて！ *tsuka-ma'ete*

thief 泥棒 *doroboo*	**robber** 強盗 *gootoo*	**molester** 痴漢 *chikan*	**pervert** 変質者 *henshitsu-sha*
pickpocket スリ *suri*	**con artist** サギ師 *sagi-shi*	**intruder** 侵入者 *shin'nyuu-sha*	**stalker** ストーカー *sutookaa*

report to the police 交番に届ける *kooban ni todokeru*

report to the station 駅に届ける *eki ni todokeru*

attacked 襲われた *osowa-reta*	**stolen** 盗まれた *nusuma-reta*	**tricked** だまされた *damasa-reta*
threatened 脅迫された *kyoohaku sareta*	**followed** つけられた *tsuke-rareta*	**overcharged** ボラれた *bora-reta*
forget/left 忘れた *wasu-reta*	**lost** なくした *naku-shita*	**dropped** 落とした *oto-shita*

wallet/purse 財布 *saifu*	**cash** 現金 *genkin*	**bag** カバン *kaban*	**passport** パスポート *pasupooto*	**camera** カメラ *kamera*

photo ID 写真入り身分証明書 *shashin iri mibun shoomee-sho*	**resident card** 在留カード *zairyuu kaado*	**cash card** キャッシュカード *kyasshu kaado*	**credit card** クレジットカード *kurejitto kaado*

トラブル

(78) Japanese can be quite rude in public places. They bump into each other, stare at each other, and walk away without even saying, "Excuse me." (公共の場での日本人のマナーは問題。人にぶつかっても「すみません」すら言わない人もいる)

Emergencies トラブル

Stop it. やめて（下さい） *yamete (kudasai)*	using me 私を利用する *watashi o ri'yoo-suru*	harassement 嫌がらせ *iya-garase*
tell lies ウソをつく *uso o tsuku*	"on-the-train" violence 車内暴力 *shanai booryoku*	sexual harassment セクハラ *seku-hara*

I didn't do it. やってません *yatte-masen*	Believe me. 信じて（下さい） *shinjite (kudasai)*	false accusation 言いがかり *iigakari*
Get me a translator. 通訳をつけて（下さい） *tsuuyaku o tsukete (kudasai)*		Get me a lawyer. 弁護士をつけて（下さい） *bengo-shi o tsukete (kudasai)*

traffic accident 交通事故 *kootsuu jiko*	police 警察 *keesatsu* Dial 110.	police officer 警察官 *keesatsu-kan*	ambulance 救急車 *kyuukyuu-sha* Dial 119.
Are you okay? 大丈夫ですか？ *daijoobu des-ka*		I'm okay. 大丈夫です *daijoobu des*	I have insurace. 保険に入ってます *hoken ni haitte-mas*
(Please) contact my family 家族に連絡して（下さい） *kazoku ni renraku shite (kudasai)*		address & phone number 連絡先 *renraku-saki*	name 名前 *nama'e*

It's my fault. 私のミスです *watashi no misu des*	* I apologize. すみません / ごめんなさい *sumimasen / gomen'nasai*

earthquake 地震 *jishin*	"Tsunami" tidal waves 津波 *tsunami*	typhoon 台風 *taifuu*	fire 火事 *kaji*

* Japan is an "apology-first" culture. A sincere and timely apology goes a long way if you want to settle legal matters out of court. (日本は「ごめんなさい社会」。心をこめてすぐに謝罪しておくと、裁判沙汰も示談ですませやすくなる)

Family & Romance
家族・人間関係・恋愛
kazoku / ningen-kankee / ren'ai

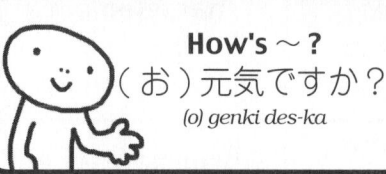

How's ～?	your family	my family
(お)元気ですか？	あなたの家族	私の家族
(o) genki des-ka	*anata no kazoku*	*watashi no kazoku*

father	mother	grandfather	grandmother
父	母	おじいさん	おばあさん
chichi	*haha*	*ojii-san*	*obaa-san*
big brother	**big sister**	**little brother**	**little sister**
兄	姉	弟	妹
ani	*ane*	*otooto*	*imooto*
husband	**wife**	**dad**	**mom**
主人	奥さん	お父さん	お母さん
shujin	*oku-san*	*ottoo-san*	*okaa-san*
child	**son**	**daughter**	**pet**
子供	息子	娘	ペット
kodomo	*musuko*	*musume*	*petto*
uncle	**aunt**	**relative**	**cousin**
おじさん	おばさん	親戚	いとこ
oji-san	*oba-san*	*shinseki*	*itoko*

Doing fine, thank you.	What's his/her name?	How old is he/she?	How many brothers/sisters?
おかげさまで	お名前は？	おいくつ(ですか)？	何人兄弟？
okage-sama de	*onama'e wa*	*oikutsu (des-ka)*	*nan-nin kyoodai*

Where do you(does he/she) live?	****** living together	living alone
お住まいは？	同居	ひとり暮らし
osumai wa	*dookyo*	*hitori-gurashi*

恋愛・家族・人間関係・

80 Japanese use many more words to describe family members depending on the degree of respect they wish to show. Ask you Japanese friend. (日本語にはこれ以外にも家族を表わす言葉が数多くある。日本人の友達に聞いてみよう)

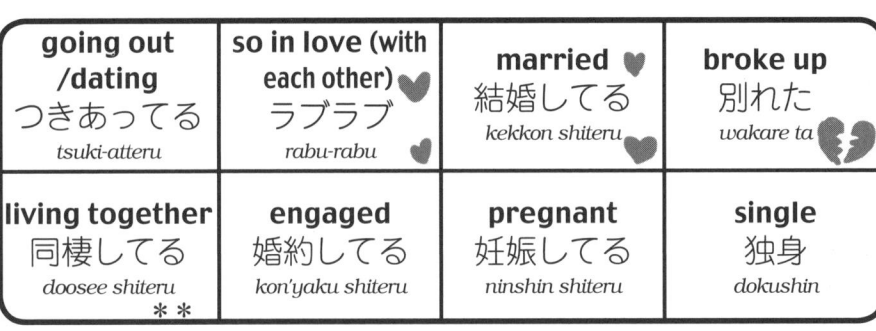

Other / その他

friend 友達 *tomodachi*	**best friend** 親友 *shin'yuu*	**acquaintance** 知り合い *shiri'ai*	**childhood friend** 幼なじみ *osana-najimi*
girl/boy friend 恋人 *koi-bito*	**boyfriend** 彼氏 / カレシ *kareshi*	**girlfriend** 彼女 / カノジョ *kanojo*	**lover/mistress** 愛人 *ai-jin*
going out /dating つきあってる *tsuki-atteru*	**so in love (with each other)** ラブラブ *rabu-rabu*	**married** 結婚してる *kekkon shiteru*	**broke up** 別れた *wakare ta*
living together 同棲してる *doosee shiteru* **	**engaged** 婚約してる *kon'yaku shiteru*	**pregnant** 妊娠してる *ninshin shiteru*	**single** 独身 *dokushin*

How did you meet your wife/husband (boy/girlfriend)?
なれ初めは？
naresome wa

How did you meet him/her? *(for friends, acquaintances, etc.)*
どういう知り合い？
dooyuu shiri'ai

same club 同じサークル *onaji saakuru*	**A friend introduced us.** 友達の紹介 *tomodachi no shookai*	**same company** 同じ会社 *onaji kaisha*	**same school** 同じ学校 *onaji gakkoo*
neighbor 近所の人 *kinjo no hito*	**Internet** インターネット *intaanetto* → P.84	**look good together** お似合い *oni'ai*	**ill-matched** 不釣合い *futsuri'ai*

argument/fight ケンカ *kenka*	**reconciliation** 仲直り *naka-na'ori*	**separation** 別居 *bekkyo*	**divorce** 離婚 *rikon*

Family & Romance

** "Doosee" is only used for an unmarried couple living together. If you have a roommate, say "dookyo" not "doosee" or people will get the wrong idea. (「同棲」と「同居」の違いに注意。ルームメイトなのに「同棲」と言うと誤解の元だ)

On the Phone, Etc

電話・ヘアカット
denwa / he'a-katto

Hello. もしもし *moshi-moshi*	**Is this the *Toyota* residence?** 豊田さんのお宅ですか？ *Toyota-san no otaku des-ka*
This is *John* speaking. ジョンと申します *jon to mooshi-mas*	**Can I speak to *Manami*-san, please?** 真奈美さんをお願いします *manami-san o onegai shimas*
Hello, is this *Manami*-san? もしもし、真奈美さん？ *moshi-moshi manami-san*	**Is this *Toyota*-san?** 豊田さんですか？ *toyota-san des-ka*

I dialed the wrong number. 間違えました *machiga'e-mashita*	**Sorry to have bothered you.** 失礼しました *shitsuree shimashita*	**She/He's out.** 出かけています *dekakete-imas*	**She/He's not home.** 留守です *rusu des*

This is *John* from *England*. イングランドのジョンです *igirisu no jon des*	**When is she/he coming back?** 何時ごろ帰りますか？ *nan-ji goro ka'erimas-ka*

It's been a long time. 久しぶり *hisashi-buri*	**How's everything?** 元気？ *genki*	**I'd like to leave a message.** 伝言をお願いします *dengon o onegai shimas*

Can we talk now? 今、平気？ *ima, heeki*	**See ya.** それじゃ、また *soreja, mata*	**Please call me back.** 電話下さい *den'wa, kudasai*	**I'll call again.** また電話します *mata den'wa shimas*

I'll be late. 遅れます *okure-mas*	**I can't find the place.** 場所がわからない *basho ga wakaranai*	**Excuse me.** すみません *sumimasen*
Where are you now? 今どこ？ *ima, doko*	**Can you find the place?** 場所わかる？ *basho, wakaru*	**Where am I/are we?** ここはどこ（ですか）？ *koko wa doko (des-ka)*

Do I need? 必要ですか？ *hitsuyoo des-ka*	**area code** 市外局番 *shigai kyoku-ban*	**How do I call overseas?** 国際電話のかけ方は？ *kokusai den'wa no kake kata wa*

82 * Japanese hairstylists may not be so good with naturally curly hair. Ask a friend to help you find the right hairstylist. (日本のヘアサロンは天然パーマ気味の髪質が苦手な場合も。日本人の友達に聞いてあなた向けの店を探そう)

Other そ の 他

Is there a good ~ ?
いい所ない？
ii tokoro, nai

* **hair salon**
ヘアサロン
he'a saron

* **barbershop**
床屋
toko-ya

aesthetic salon
エステ
esute

Do I need a reservation?
予約は必要（ですか）？
yoyaku wa hitsuyoo (des-ka)

How long is the wait?
どの位、待ちますか？
dono-kurai, machimas-ka

How much?
いくら（ですか）？
ikura (des-ka)

haircut カット *katto*	perm パーマ *paama*	hair coloring ヘアカラー *he'a karaa*
shampoo シャンプー *shampuu*	shave 顔剃り *ka'o-sori*	Please give me ~ . お願いします *onegai shimas*

this part
ここを
koko o

entire part
全体を
zentai o

short ショート *shooto*	medium ミディアム *midi'amu*	long ロング *rongu*
"shaggy" シャギー *shagii*	spiky ツンツン *tsun-tsun*	wavy ウェーブ *weebu*
straight ストレート *sutoreeto*	layered レイヤー *reiyaa*	curled カール *kaaru*

On the Phone, Etc.

"What's the latest trend?" —— *"Ima no hayari wa?"*

** **I want it cut this much.**
この位カットして
kono-kurai katto shite

I want the hairstyle in this photo.
この写真のようにお願い
kono shashin no yooni onegai

** Japanese hairstylists will ask how many centimeters of your hair you want trimmed. I hope it isn't too confusing for my American readers. （日本では何センチ単位での髪の切り方を指定しがちだ。インチに慣れたアメリカ人読者が心配だ…）

Keeping in Touch
連絡先の交換 *renraku-saki no kookan*

Can I have your ~ ? 教えて下さい *oshi'ete kudasai*	full name 氏名 *shimee*	address 住所 *juusho*
Please write it down. 書いて下さい *kaite kudasai*	email address メールアドレス *meeru adoresu*	telephone number 電話番号 *den'wa bangoo*

MEMO

Twitter
ツイッター
tsuittaa

Facebook
フェイスブック
feesu-bukku

Instagram
インスタグラム
insuta-guramu

Let's keep in touch.
連絡取り合おう
renraku tori-a'oo

連絡先の交換

I'll write to you. 手紙書きます *tegami, kakimas*	I'll send you. 送ります *okurimas*	Please send me. 送って下さい *okutte kudasai*
Please write to me. 手紙下さい *tegami, kudasai*	thank-you note お礼の手紙 *oree no tegami*	photograph 写真 *shashin*
I'll email you. メールします *meeru shimas*		Please email me. メールして下さい *meeru shite kudasai*
I'll miss you. 名残惜しいです *nagori-oshii des*		I'll come again. また来ます *mata kimas*

This is my address and phone number. 私の連絡先です *watashi no renraku-saki des*	* Please come and see me. 遊びに来て下さい *asobi ni kite kudasai*

(84) * When Japanese use this phrase, they are usually just being polite. If they don't give you a specific date and time, don't "drop in." (日本人が日時の指定なしで言う「遊びに来て」に注意。本当に行くと、かなり困られたりする)

Section 2
第2部

Tips on Understanding Japanese People
日本人を理解するためのヒント

I hope you're having fun with the "POINT-AND-SPEAK" method. As you grow used to the way Japanese people speak, you will gradually gain a better understanding of what they're saying. But if you have any trouble grasping why Japanese people say what they say, maybe you should learn some more keywords to understand what makes them tick. Read on, as I have some tips for you.

第一部の指さしシートはいかがでしたか？ 慣れるにつれて、だんだんと日本人の言葉が聞き取れるようになってきたのではないでしょうか。このセクションでは、さらに日本語がわかるようになりたい人のために、日本人を理解するためのキーワードを取り上げて説明していきたいと思います。

apology (謝罪 / *shazai*)

Japan's "apology-first" culture makes it possible for foreigners to get out of most jams with "sumimasen." "Sumimasen", as shown on P.8, is equivalent to "Excuse me." It is, however, just as useful for apologies and some Japanese prefer to say "sumimasen" as they think it is a more refined apology "for grown-ups" than "gomen'nasai." Saying "sumimasen" is also a clever way for non-Japanese speakers to hide their limited vocabulary.

日本の文化は謝罪してナンボのところがある。日本語の苦手なガイジンさんはまず「すみません」という言葉を覚えるとよい。「すみません」という言葉は、相手の注意を引く言葉（P.8を参照）であると同時に、謝罪の表現でもある。ちなみに「すみません」は「ごめんなさい」よりも、社会人向けのこなれた謝罪の言葉だと考えている日本人もいる。日本語を話さない人にとって使いでのあるフレーズだ。日本語がよくわからない場合も、「すみません」というとりあえずの一言は有効なわけだし。

appearance' sake (見栄 / *mi'e*)

A lot of Japanese will do anything for "mi'e." In a culture where silence is "golden," appearance speaks much louder than words. Japanese people's "mi'e" is usually reflected in the clothes they wear and the cars they drive. Some even skimp on food so they will have enough money for "mi'e" needs.

大変な思いをしてまで見栄を張る日本人は多い。「沈黙が金」とされる文化であるが故に、言葉よりも見かけが重要になりがちだからだ。日本人がどれだけ見栄を張っているかは、その人の洋服と車に反映されがちだ。中には見栄を張るための予算を捻出すべく、食費を切りつめる人もいるほどだ。

average / being an average person (普通 / *futsuu*)

In a society where "the nail that sticks up gets hammered down," people work hard to be "futsuu(average)". When they feel they know each other a little better, it's usually okay to be more individualistic. The important thing is to show that you're not an annoying "nail" that keeps sticking up.

日本では「出る杭は打たれる」。だからこそ「普通」であるための努力が大切になる。自分らしさをアピールするには、まずは少しずつお互いを知り合うというのがルールなのだ。大切なのは、和を乱し続ける「杭」ではない事をアピールすることだ。

consideration (気配り / *kikubari*)

Being considerate is a virtue in Japanese culture, where people live in small apartments, commute in jam-packed trains and work in cramped offices. But being considerate at all times is hard. This sometimes makes people insensitive to situations where "kikubari" is more a must than a virtue.

手狭なアパートに住んでいる人が、電車にギュウギュウ詰めになって通勤して、きわめて狭い会社で仕事に精を出す。そうした現実の中を生きる日本人は、気配りを美徳としている。しかし、常に気配りをしようと頑張るあまりに疲れてしまい、本当に気配りが必要な時に限って自己チューになってしまうのも日本人の現実なのだ……。

borrowed words (外来語 / *gairai-go*)

The Japanese language has incorporated so many English words that many people find it hard to talk without using English. Today's young Japanese, who grew up using more English words than any other generation, will likely have a hard time telling foreign words from Japanese words. But many still have a problem with correct English pronunciation, leaving a little niche for a phrasebook like this one.

カタカナ語として日本語の一部となっている英語は多い。どのくらい多いかと言うと、カタカナ言葉を使わないと会話が続かないという日本人も少なくないほどだ。現代の日本の若者たちは、かつてないほどに英語に埋もれて育てられた世代だけに、日本語と外来語の区別すらつかぬまま大人になってしまう人もいるだろう。しかし、どれだけ英語が日本語に侵入しようが、発音はそう簡単にうまくなるわけではない。だからこそ、この手の本を書いている人間もどうにかやっていけるわけなのである。

bowing (お辞儀 / *ojigi*)

For some Japanese, bowing is more a reflex than a custom. They were taught to bow early in life by conservative parents, trained to bow "properly" in job-seekers' workshops before leaving college, and finally conditioned to bow in job training by their "superiors" at work. Maybe this helps explain why some Japanese take a bow as they shake hands with "foreigners".

　お辞儀が体に染みついてしまっている日本人もいる。まず子供時代に両親からしっかりとしつけられ、大学の就職セミナーでトレーニングを受け、就職後には会社の上司からトドメのお辞儀教育を受けるのだ。ガイジンさんと握手をする際にも体が反応してしまう人たちが、どのようにして生み出されるのかわかってもらえるだろうか。

blondes and redheads
(金髪と茶髪/*kimpatsu to chapatsu*)

　Most Japanese blondes and redheads go to hair salons to have their hair dyed. Hair coloring has become such a big fad among "cool" Japanese that it is becoming increasingly rare to find "cool" people with nice, black hair. I have my hair still nice and black, but whether my friends think I'm cool is another story.

　流行に敏感な日本人は、髪を染めることで個性やカッコよさを表現しようとしている。日本で見かける金髪や茶髪のほとんどは、わざわざ染めている人たちなのである。しかし、ここまで染めるのが一般的になってくると、逆に個性的でカッコいい黒髪の持ち主に出会うのが貴重になってくる。ちなみに私は日本人ならではの黒髪のままだが、私がカッコいいかどうかはまた別の次元の話ではある。

comic books (マンガ/*manga*)

　In many countries comic books are for children. In Japan, however, there is a big market for adult "manga." Some of them are sexually explicit and a lot of international visitors are shocked to see polite, well-dressed Japanese gentlemen reading such comics on buses and trains. Some convenience stores sell even more hardcore "adult manga." If you're curious, check out the far edge of the book section where there are always a few men browsing. Maybe you'll see me there too.

　マンガは子供向けの娯楽だという国も多いだろう。しかし日本という国は、大人向けのマンガが売れる国なのだ。大人向けのマンガには、性的描写がハッキリと描かれているものもあり、それを真面目そうな日本の紳士が電車やバスで読む姿は、海外から来た人にショックを与えることも多いようだ。コンビニではさらに過激な「アダルトマンガ」が売られていることもある。興味がある人は、いつも男ども数人がタカっ

ている辺りをチェックしてみよう。私の姿を見かけるかもしれない。

dieting （ダイエット/*dai'etto*）

Dieting has become a national pastime in fashion-conscious Japan. These days, men as well as women see maintaining a trim figure as a must. Some become such obsessive weight watchers that even the slightest blip on the scale sends them into a deep funk.

何かとオシャレにうるさい日本では、ダイエットはついに国民的流行になってしまった。女性だけではなく最近では男性までが、スリムな体型の維持に気を遣っている。中には、体重計の最小目盛り分ウェートアップしただけで、相当に精神的ダメージを受ける人もいるほどだ。

diplomatic language （建前/*tatema'e*）

When Japanese meet someone new, they usually restrict their conversation to "safe" topics. They usually make an effort to say only those things they think their new acquaintance wants to hear. Take it with a grain of salt if your brand-new Japanese friend tells you what an intelligent, good-looking person you are. (See also "hon'ne" on P.95.)

初対面の人と話す時、日本人は「安全」な内容の会話のみに終始しがちだ。知り合いになったばかりの人が喜ぶような話ばかりをしてしまうのである。そうした訳で、新しい友達から頭の良さとかルックスの良さを誉められても、あまり真に受けないようにおすすめしておく。

eye contact （視線/*shisen*）

Japanese think it is impolite to maintain eye contact for long periods. Even in the middle of a conversation, they usually look away from each other every 30 seconds or so. Some people completely avoid eye contact when they speak to someone new. Japanese also try to avoid eye contact with strangers. Eye contact between male strangers that lasts more than 5 seconds is not unlike a staring contest between two fighters at the start of a match.

A lot of Japanese also avoid eye contact when saying heart-felt words of love. They usually look away or down demurely and talk to their shoelaces. Fixing your would-be lover with a direct gaze is seen as a mark of desperation or humorous intent. These rules don't apply to Westerners, however. After seeing so many Hollywood movies Japanese have come to expect "bolder" expressions of love from "gaijin-sans." In fact, failure on your part to show sufficient romanticism could result in disaster!

日本では、相手の目をずっと見続けるのは、礼儀に欠ける行為だと考えられている。会話をしている者同士でも、30秒も目を合わせたら何となく目を逸らし合うものである。初対面の人とは、まったく目を合わせたがらない人もいる。日本人は通常、知らない人とも目を合わせようとしない。通りすがりの男性同士が5秒以上も目を合わせ続けていたら、今まさに始まらんとしている対決へのプレリュードなのである。

愛の告白の時も、目を合わせたがらない日本人が多い。目をそらすか視線を下に向けて、まるで靴ひもに話しかけているかのようなのだ。愛の告白をする際にしっかりと目を合わせると、相当飢えているのか、何かギャグでもかまそうとしていると思われがちだからだ。しかし西洋の人たちは、このルールに縛られないほうがいい。日本人はハリウッド映画から外国人の愛の表現について学んできたからだ。ガイジンさんは自分たちらしく堂々と愛を語らないと、逆に大失敗する可能性がある。

fishing for sympathy (愚痴/*guchi*)

"Guchi" is repeated complaints mixed with unspoken pleas for shows of sympathy. "Guchi" for men usually takes place at a bar, with colleagues or friends, where they commiserate over drinks. "Guchi" for women, on the other hand, can take place anywhere. One place quite popular for an exchange of "guchi" is, believe it or not, the ladies' room. Now you know why Japanese women like to go to the ladies' room with their friends.

同情して欲しいがために不満を繰り返し述べる行為を愚痴と呼ぶ。男性は大抵の場合において酒場に行き、友人や同僚と共に呑みながら愚痴をこぼし合う。女性の場合は場所を選ばずに愚痴をこぼせるようだが、とりわけ人気の高い愚痴スポットは意外にも女子トイレなんだそうだ。日本人女性は仲間同士連れ立ってトイレに行きがちだが、その訳がおわかりいただけただろうか。

gaijin / gaikoku-jin … someone from the "outside" world (外人／外国人)

For many Japanese "gaijin" simply means "someone from the outside world." But some "sensitive" foreigners in Japan feel the word is discriminatory, even when it is used in a completely neutral context. They maintain that Japanese should say "foreigner" or "gaikoku-jin." However, in the early '80s and '90s, some non-Japanese people claimed instead that "foreigner" was the bad word — as it was alienating and insensitive to their unique roots as individuals. Some said they would rather be called "gaijins." *The times, they're a-changing* and it reminds of what Bob Dylan said about people and their use of words — "There are no dirty words. There are only dirty minds." He has a point.

　日本人の多くは「外の世界の人」程度の意味で「外人」と言うが、この言葉に"差別性"を感じる"敏感な"外国人もいる。が、80年代前半〜90年代には、"正しい"言葉のはずの"foreigner"が、「疎外感を与え」「個人個人のルーツに対し無神経」だとして嫌われたこともあり、「外人」と呼ばれたほうがいいと言っていた人たちもいた。まさに『時代は変わる』であり、この曲を書いたボブ・ディランはこうも言っている――「けがらわしい言葉なんてない。けがらわしい心があるだけさ」。一理ある気がする。

healing (癒し/*iyashi*)

　"Iyashi" which translates roughly as "healing" or "healing effect" may be the most important catch phrase of the new millennium. A lot of Japanese people are so stressed keeping up with the rapid pace of change that they seek refuge in everything from kitschy key rings to uninspired pop songs reputed to have a healing effect. I read that an increasing number of Japanese tourists head for Asian travel destinations in search of "iyashi." This becomes yet another source of frustration when they encounter hoards of "iyashi-hungry" tourists like themselves at their destination. They come back home and complain of needing more "iyashi" after the holiday.

　「ヒーリング」とか「ヒーリング効果」という言葉に訳すことのできる"癒し"という言葉は、2000年代で最も重要なキーワードかもしれない。激しく変化する時代に生きる日本人たちはストレスをため込むあまりに、ファンシー系のキーホルダーだろうがしょーもないポップソングだろうが、癒し効果があるとうたわれていると、つい飛びつかずにはいられないようなのだ。私が読んだ記事によれば、癒しを求めてアジアを目指すツーリストが増えているそうだ。しかし、アジアに癒しを求めて旅立ったのはいいが、旅先で癒しに飢えた他の日本人ツーリストばかりを見かけ、またしてもストレスをため込むなんてこともあるという。そんな癒し系ツアーから帰国した人は、休暇のおかげで疲れたから新しい「癒し」が必要だなんてこぼすのである。

"Japlish" (日本人英語/*nihon-jin eego*)

　I could write a whole book on this topic alone. English education is compulsory in Japan for all secondary students, but relatively few actually learn to speak it. And it's no wonder when their teachers are often poor speakers as well. When you meet Japanese for the first time, laughing at their "Japlish" could ruin a potential friendship.

このトピックに関してなら、さらに1冊本が書ける。日本では中学から英語が必修科目となるが、ちゃんと話せるようになる生徒はほとんどいない。それもそのはずで、英語をまともに話せる英語の先生があまりいないのだ。初対面の日本人が話す英語を馬鹿にすると、せっかく芽生えかけた友情が台無しになる恐れがあるので注意。

losing one's temper (キレる/*kireru*)

This is usually what happens when Japanese find themselves at the very end of their "gaman (patience)." You may have heard of a few incidents where teenage boys completely "snapped" and stabbed their parents to death. (Of course, they are extreme examples.) Japanese adults may be too lenient with each other's drunken misbehavior, but this can be an important stress release for Japan's overworked "corporate warriors." Thanks to the many Suntory, Kirin and Yebisu beers I enjoy, I hardly ever lose my temper.

我慢に我慢を重ねていた日本人がついに限界に達すると起こる現象、それが「キレる」だ。完全にキレてしまった結果、日本の10代の男の子が両親を刺殺してしまった事件などをご存知ないだろうか（もちろんこれは極端な「キレかた」だが）。日本人は酒の席での失敗に寛容すぎるかもしれないが、戦いに疲れた「企業戦士」のストレスにはけ口を与えるためには意味のあることなのだ。サントリー、キリン、エビスをたっくさん飲んでいるおかげで、私はメッタにキレたりすることはない。

mistreating loved ones (八つ当たり/*yatsu-atari*)

Many Japanese grow weary from all the "consideration" they have to show at the office. They could let off steam singing karaoke, but sometimes singing and drinking aren't quite enough. When they need to vent, they tend to take it out on the ones they love. If the other person also needs to vent, "yatsu-atari" usually leads to a heated shouting match with no winners.

会社で「気配り」をするがあまりに、精神的に疲れてしまう日本人も多い。カラオケでストレス発散といきたいが、時には飲めや歌えやだけでは気持ちが晴れないこともある。そんな時に日本人はどうするのか？ 家族や恋人などへの八つ当たりである。八つ当たりされた人もちょうど八つ当たりしたい気分だったりすると、争いはやがて勝者なき怒鳴り合いへと発展してゆく。

Nihon or Nippon?
(ニホンかニッポンか？/*nihon ka nippon ka*)

Japanese usually call Japan "Nihon" in Japanese, but when Japanese people feel more patriotic than usual, a lot of them say "Nippon" instead of

"Nihon." Listen for chants of "Nippon" at international athletic competitions. Japanese volleyball teams usually have the loudest cheering section, which explodes with chants of "Nippon, cha-cha-cha !" every time a Japanese player scores a point. "Nippon, cha-cha-cha" sounds a lot funnier when uttered by a "gaikoku-jin" spectator rooting for Japanese athletes. Say it at the right time and you'll be the hit of the next Olympics.

　日本人は自分の国を通常「ニホン」と呼んでいるが、自分が生まれ育った国に対する気持ちが高まるにつれ、「ニホン」は「ニッポン」へと変化を遂げる。国際的なスポーツの大会では「ニッポン」コールが起きる。応援団の騒がしさで群を抜くバレーボールの大会では、日本が得点をあげるごとに爆発的な音量の「ニッポン、チャ、チャ、チャ」コールが聞かれる。この「ニッポン、チャ、チャ、チャ」だが、ガイジンさんが言うとものすごくおかしな響きとなる。うまいタイミングで言えば、次のオリンピックでは人気者になること請け合いだ。

platform "pizza"
（プラットホーム・ピザ / *puratto-hoomu piza*）

　This is not the latest trend in Japanese fast food. This is a phrase coined out by an old acquaintance of mine when he described the vomit left by a drunken company man on a JR Yamanote Line platform. Japanese people are quite tolerant of drunken misbehavior, with the possible exception of sexual harassment. A lot of Japanese people think that the more stressed you are from overwork, the more drunken misbehavior you're likely to get into. Should you overdrink and "deliver some platform pizza," report to work on schedule the following morning, "apologize" and work longer hours than usual for the next few days. You'll most likely be "forgiven" and your "platform pizza" forgotten. Take it from me. I did it a couple of times when I was younger, and my boss still kept me on the payroll.

　日本で流行のファーストフードの話ではない。酔っ払ったサラリーマンがJR山の手線のホームに残したゲロを見て、私の古い知り合いがふと漏らした言葉である。日本人は酒の席での失敗に寛容で、問題になるとしたらセクハラ行為くらいだろう。と言うのも、真面目に働いてストレスをためている人ほど、酒の席では乱れてしまうものだと考えている日本人が多いからだ。飲み過ぎて「プラットホーム・ピザのデリバリー」をしてしまった場合だが、翌日は遅刻せずに出勤したら何はなくともまず「謝罪」し、それから数日間はこれまでよりもさらに会社に残って働くことだ。大抵の場合において罪は許され、「ピザ」をぶんまいた事は忘れてもらえる。私も若かりし頃は何度かやってしまっているが、それでも首を切られるような事態にはならなかった。

patience (我慢/*gaman*)

"Gaman" may be one Japanese virtue that a lot of foreigners have trouble understanding. If you want to find out what "gaman" is all about, eat "natto" every morning, spend 3 hours round-trip on a jam-packed train and bow at least 200 times a day. Then you will begin to know why Japanese had to make a virtue out of it.

日本的な美徳のひとつに「我慢」というものがあるが、これを理解できるガイジンさんは少なかろう。「我慢」というものが一体どのようなものか知りたかったら、毎朝納豆を食べて、満員電車で往復3時間かけて通勤し、1日最低でも200回はお辞儀をする生活をしてみるとよい。なぜ日本人が「我慢」を美徳とせざるを得なかったか、きっとわかるはずだから。

public eye (社会の目/*shakai no me*)

Japanese people are not used to doing what they want to do when they are in "the public eye." Suppose a drunken "company man" drops his wallet when he hurries off a subway at Ginza Station. A "gaijin-san", whether he chooses to pocket it or hand it to a station official, wouldn't hesitate to pick it right up. But the average Japanese would become so self-conscious in "the public eye," he wouldn't even have second thoughts about darting a second glance at the wallet. Maybe you have heard about lost wallets and purses returned to the owners without missing a yen in Japan. The way I see it, it has more to do with people's self-consciousness than with the their personal integrity.

「社会の目」があると自分のしたいように振る舞えない——それが日本人という生き物だ。たとえば、酔ったサラリーマンが銀座駅で地下鉄を降りた拍子に、財布を落としたとしよう。それを見つけたのがガイジンさんなら、駅員に届けるにしろ中身を失敬するにせよ、周囲を意識することなく拾い上げることができるはずだ。ところが日本人ときたら「社会の目」を気にするあまりに、自分が周囲からどう見られるかを意識せずにはいられないのだ。日本で財布を落としても、中身が無事なまま持ち主に戻るなんて話を聞いたことがないだろうか。日本人が正直だという以上に、自意識過剰なせいだからではないかと、私はかねがね思っているのだが。

real intention (本音/*hon'ne*)

"Hon'ne," or real intent, is the opposite of "tatema'e (See "tatema'e" on P.89). Japanese often cover up their "hon'ne" when they are still in early stages of a new relationship. They usually think it's the best policy to humor the other person along to better build the relationship. They think it is much more "polite" because their "hon'ne" could make the other person unhappy. A Japanese salesman may tell you he is a "Ham Fighters" fan himself (See "Ham Fighters" on P.52) when he finds out you have a season ticket for the "Hams." But his "hon'ne" may be that he is a hardcore Tigers fan from Osaka and doesn't give a #&$! about "those miserable Hams." When a new Japanese acquaintance tells you something nice about what you do, take it with a large grain of salt. I always do when I test-market my phrasebook to Japanese readers. They will say "What a nice phrasebook by such a nice author!" but start to laugh at the typos the moment my back is turned!

「本音」はその人の心の奥底を表わす言葉で、「建前（89ページを参照）」の反対に位置する言葉だ。新しい人間関係が始まったばかりのうちは、日本人は「本音」を隠して相手に調子を合わせ、相手を良い気分にさせながら人間関係を築き上げようとする。たとえば、あなたが"ハムと戦う男たち（P.52を参照）"のシーズン・チケットを買うほどの大ファンだと知った、日本人の営業マンがいたとしよう。彼はきっと「私もハムと戦う男たちを応援してますよ」くらいの事は平気で言うだろう。じつは大阪出身の筋金入り阪神ファンだったとしても、本音では「あのどうしょーもねぇハムども」なんて思っていたとしても、である。知り合いになったばかりの日本人に誉められた場合は、眉にたっぷり唾をつけて聞いておこう。日本人読者が自分の本にどんな反応をするか、テストする際の私がそうである。「筆者も素敵な方だし、本の内容も素敵」なんて言ってくれても、背中を向けた瞬間に誤植を指さして笑われるのがオチなのだから。

reserve and restraint （遠慮/enryo）

When visiting the home of a new Japanese friend, don't make yourself at home too soon. Your host will likely tell you to make yourself comfortable, but try to practice some "enryo" to make a good impression. When presented with fancy Japanese sweets, "well-mannered" Japanese look away from them with an appreciative smile and try not to think about it for at least a few minutes. When your host offers them for the third or fourth time, it is finally OK for them to dig in. Don't be too embarrassed if your stomach growls. It has happened to me and it happens to "well-mannered" Japanese too.

新しく友達になったばかりの日本人の家に招かれた時の注意だ。「ご自分の家のつもりでどうぞ」とでも言われるだろうが、待ってましたとばかりにくつろいでしまうのは考えものだ。良い印象を残すには、多少は「遠慮」することを覚えよう。美しい和

菓子をだされた場合、マナーの良い日本人がどう振る舞うか知ってるだろうか？ まず感謝の笑みを浮かべてお菓子から目をそらし、その後数分間はお菓子のことを考えないように努力し、3度目か4度目にすすめられて初めて手をつけるのだ。お腹が鳴ってしまった場合でも、あまり気にしないように。私自身それで失敗したこともあるし、私よりマナーのある日本人もそんな失敗をすることがある。

rock, paper, scissors （ジャンケン/janken）

"Janken" is what Japanese people do instead of a tossup. People make the shape of a rock ("guu"), scissors ("choki") or paper (paa) with their fingers. "Guu" is a clenched fist and wins over "choki." "Choki" is the "peace" sign and wins over "paa." "Paa" is an open hand and wins over "guu." When two "janken" contestants make identical signs, it is a draw and they do another round to decide the winner. When there are more than three participants with three different signs, that's a three-way tie and they keep doing round after round of "janken" until they have one final winner. In the land of "enryo" and "kikubari" people need "the fairness of janken" to decide who will eat the last Japanese sweet on the plate. Sometimes a dozen rounds of janken must be performed for the prize of a tiny "manju" bun.

何かを決める際にコイントスはしない日本人だが、ジャンケンはよくやる。「グー」は握りこぶし、「チョキ」はピースサイン、「パー」は手を開いた形である。「グー」は「チョキ」に勝ち、「チョキ」は「パー」に勝ち、「パー」は「グー」に勝つ。相手と同じ形を出してしまったら「あいこ」となり、勝負がつくまでジャンケンを続ける。3人以上でジャンケンをした際に「あいこ」が続くと、勝ち残りの勝者が決まるまで何ラウンドもジャンケンが続く。「遠慮」と「気配り」の国、日本では、ジャンケンのようなフェアな勝者決定システムは、皿に残った最後の和菓子が誰の胃袋に収まるかを決める上でも重要なのだ。時には小さなまんじゅう1つのために、12ラウンドものジャンケンが行なわれることもある。

"salaryman" and "OL"
(サラリーマンとOL/sararii-man to oo'eru)

Quite a lot of Japanese workers work for a monthly salary and are given the "Japlish" title of "salaryman." Most "salarymen" are "company men" who become quite stressed from being what they are. "OL" stands for "office lady" and has become the most popular word to describe female office workers. Quite a lot of them work even harder than "salarymen" and get even better results. Some "salarymen" who become even more stressed from seeing "OLs" outperforming them in the office, may visit special "massage parlors" and get their favorite "masseurs" to dress up in "OL" outfits so they can somehow make up for their feelings of inferiority at work.

　毎月のサラリーのために仕事をしている日本人は数多く、彼らには「サラリーマン」という呼称が与えられている。「サラリーマン」の多くが「会社人間」であることを余儀なくされているため、かなりストレスをためながら仕事をしている。ＯＬは「オフィスレディー」の略で、オフィスで働く女性を表わす言葉として最も一般的なものだ。「サラリーマン」よりも仕事熱心なＯＬも多く、男性よりも結果を出すＯＬも少なくはない。それを目の当たりにした「サラリーマン」の中には、女性に負けたことでさらにストレスを感じる人もいる。彼らの中には、"特別な"マッサージ店に行ってお気に入りのマッサージ嬢に"ＯＬルック"をしてもらい、とりあえずバーチャルな形で劣等感を克服している人もいるようなのだ。

seniority system （年功序列/*nenkoo-joretsu*)

A rule of thumb for understanding Japan's seniority system. People treat those who are older and more experienced with greater respect as they put in more time at the company. Older people, who take it for granted that they are entitled to respect from younger people, often have trouble working with younger bosses with more computer skills.

　年功序列の考え方では、年齢が上の人や経験が長い人が「会社により長く貢献してきた人」と見なされ、若い人や経験が浅い人よりも大事に扱われる。そのため年配者の中には、年齢が上である以上は若い連中から敬われて当然と考える人もいる。が、そういう人たちが自分よりもコンピューターに詳しい年下の上司の下に配属されると、とても困るハメになるのである。

sentences without a subject
（主語のない文章/*shugo no nai bunshoo*)

In Japanese you can delete the subject of a sentence and still make yourself understood. For example, where English speakers would say, "I am hungry," Japanese would just say "Hungry." and still understand "who" is hungry. Japanese people are so good at "sensing" the right meaning from the context that they hardly ever have any trouble knowing the omitted subject of a sentence. At times Japanese even delete the subject and object of a sentence and still understand each other. Where English speakers would say "I need it," Japanese would simply say "Hitsuyoo (Need)" and still know "who" needs "what." While this may sound quite confusing for non-Japanese, the key here is for you to say the key word. They will complete the rest of the sentence in their heads and will most likely understand you. Got it?

文中の主語を省略しても、ちゃんと意味が通じる言葉、それが日本語である。例えば、英語では「私はおなかがすいた」と言わなければならないだろうが、日本語の場合は「おなかがすいた」と言うだけで、誰が空腹なのかわかるのである。日本人は文脈から正しい意味を「感じ取る」のが得意で、省略された主語を何の問題もなく知ってしまう人たちなのだ。時には、主語どころか目的語まで省略するが、それでも平気で理解してしまう。英語ならば「私はそれが必要です」と言わなければならなくとも、日本語では単に「必要」と言うだけで、誰が何を必要としているのかわかってしまうのである。外国人にはかなり難しいかもしれないが、とにかくキーワードを言えば良いと覚えておこう。文章の残りの部分は、それを聞いた日本人が頭の中で勝手に組み立てて、かなりの確立で言いたい事を理解してくれるはずだ。アナタ ハ ソレヲ リカイ シマシタ カ？

sexual harassment (セクハラ/*seku-hara*)

"Seku-hara" or "sexual harassment" has more or less become "the most unpardonable misconduct" in Japan. A casual pat by a male boss on the shoulder of his female subordinate can be an act of "seku-hara," if it makes her uncomfortable. Reverse sexual harassment, where women make men uncomfortable, isn't quite as big a problem. I was drinking with a woman I know who made a big case out of my beer belly. When I joked that I would sue her, she told me she wanted it settled out of court and bought me another beer. "Seku-hara" isn't all bad, I thought.

日本で「今いちばん許し難い行為」の座についているのは「セクハラ」である。「セクハラ」とは「セクシャルハラスメント」のことだ。たとえば男性上司が女性の部下の肩をポンと叩いたとしよう。この「ポンッ」が女性の部下を不快な気持ちにさせたら、これは立派なセクハラ行為と取られかねないのである。女性が男性を不快な気持ちにさせると逆セクハラになるが、こちらのほうはそこまでは問題視されていない。私は一緒に飲んでいた女性に、ビール腹のことで随分と色々言われたことがあるが、「訴えるわよ！」とジョークで返したら示談をもちかけられ、彼女のおごりでもう一杯飲めることになったこともある。セクハラといっても悪いことばかりじゃないのだ。

shortening long words (言葉を縮める/kotoba o chijimeru)

Japanese don't use many acronyms. What they do instead is to condense long words and phrases into 3-or-4 letter words. セクシャルハラスメント ("Sexual harassment") becomes セクハラ ("Seku-hara"). コンビニエンスストア ("Convenience store") becomes コンビニ ("Combini"). パーソナルコンピューター ("Personal computer") becomes パソコン ("Pasocom"). Even a short name like Brad Pitt (ブラッドピット) becomes BraPi （ブラピ). Many shortened words have become very much a part of the language. Good news for BraPi.

日本人は頭文字を集めた略語（BBC、WWFなど）はそれほど使わないが、長い言葉や表現を3〜4文字に短縮するのが好きだ。セクシャルハラスメントはセクハラ、コンビニエンスストアはコンビニ、パーソナルコンピューターはパソコンといった具合で、ブラッドピット程度の短い名前でも「ブラピ」になってしまう。しかし、こうして短縮化される場合、言語の壁を越えた外来語が広く受け入れられて、日本語の一部となった証しでもある。「ブラピ」にとっては名誉なことだ。

silly puns (usually made by old men)
(オヤジギャグ/oyaji gyagu)

Japanese people love to laugh, but their sense of humor is quite different from generation to generation. Old men generally love making puns. They think their puns are so funny that they can't help telling them to younger people. Young people may smile politely, but a lot of them hate those "silly" puns and "freeze up" when you mention "oyaji gyagu" or "old men's puns."

日本人は笑うことが大好きだが、面白いと感じるものは世代によって千差万別だ。歳のいった男性は語呂合わせを好む傾向があり、自分で考えたギャグに酔うあまりに、若者の前で披露してくれることがある。若者たちはしかたなく笑顔を浮かべたりもするが、実のところそうしたつまらない語呂合わせが大嫌いだったりする。中には「オヤジギャグ」の話をしただけで、「凍り付く」若者もいるほどである。

sleeping on the train (電車で居眠り/densha de inemuri)

A lot of Japanese workers fall asleep on the train home from work. They are usually very tired after working long hours at the office. Of course you can laugh at the way they move back and forth with the jolts and jerks of the train, but be ready to witness a magically well-timed awakening. Believe it or not, most "train snoozers" wake up just in time to get off at the right station without ever using the alarm function on their wristwatches.

　帰りの電車の中で居眠りをする日本人は多い。会社で長時間働いたせいで疲れている人が多いからだ。電車の揺れに合わせて揺れる居眠りジャパニーズを見て笑っているうちに、ガイジンさんたちは驚異的な出来事を目の当たりにすることになる。「電車居眠り族」たちは自分の駅が近づくと、腕時計のアラームを使うことすらなく、絶妙なタイミングで目を覚ますのだ。信じられるかな？

things Japanese （日本的なもの/*nihon-teki na mono*）

　If it weren't for the international tourists visiting Japan, Japanese customs and traditions may be gradually forgotten by contemporary Japan.　Many Japanese people think that "cross-cultural" communication means talking to non-Japanese visitors about Japan in English, so they try hard to talk about things in English that they don't even talk about in Japanese.　And THEY discover Japan.

　ガイジンさんが日本に来てくれなくなったら、日本的な習慣や伝統は次第に忘れ去られてしまうかもしれない。「異文化コミュニケーション」＝「外国から来た人たちに英語で日本を紹介すること」だと考えている日本人は多く、普段は母国語ですら話さないような事柄を英語で語るべく奮闘する。その結果、日本の心を発見するのは、ガイジンさんではなく当の日本人たちだったりするのである。

trying too hard （頑張る/*gambaru*）

　No word can better describe the spirit of Japanese industriousness than "gambaru."　"Gambaru," which is often translated as "trying one's best," is actually more like "trying too hard" or "trying harder than one needs to."　Even if they fail to get results, Japanese find much comfort in the act of trying.　So much so that they see it as a virtue in and of itself.　Some put so much into "trying" that they have little energy left for the task at hand.

　日本人の勤勉さを表わす言葉といったら、やはり「頑張る」につきる。「頑張る」という言葉はよく「ベストをつくす」という意味の英語に訳されるが、実際には「頑張りすぎる」とか「必要以上に努力する」といったニュアンスに近い感じだ。結果が出せなくとも、頑張った事に対して満足することもできるのが日本人なのであり、頑張るという行為自体が美徳とされているほどだ。中には「頑張る」という行為に対して頑張り過ぎるがあまりに、実際の仕事に向けるべきエネルギーを枯渇させてしまう人もいたりする。

wordiness (くどい/*kudoi*)

Remember to be "wordy" when you ask for directions in English. Suppose you want to go to Yamashita-koen in Yokohama. If you already know that "koen" is the Japanese word for "park," you might want to avoid wordiness by cutting "koen" out and say "Yamashita Park." But many Japanese won't understand because they say "Yamashita-koen" all the time. Say "Yamashita-koen Park," "Ara-kawa River," "Kototoi-bashi Bridge," etc. to help them understand you. When you converse in Japanese, however, try to be concise. Not many Japanese like wordy people. Oh, you think I'm too wordy? Well, I guess I will stop talking before they boo me off stage.

　英語で道をたずねなければならない時には、くどい位の物の言い方をしておこう。横浜の山下公園に行く場合を例として説明するが、"park"という意味のある"koen（公園）"という言葉を入れて言うかどうかが勝負の分かれ目なのだ。「ヤマシタ・コーエン・パーク」というと「公園」という意味の言葉がダブってしまうため、気を利かせて「ヤマシタ・パーク」と言うと、逆に地元民には理解しにくい言葉になってしまうことも多いようだ。山下公園は「ヤマシタ・コーエン・パーク」、荒川は「アラカワ・リバー」、「言問橋」は「コトトイバシ・ブリッジ」と言っておくのが安全だ。が、日本語で話す際には、簡潔に必要な言葉だけ言うのがいい。日本人はくどい物言いの人を歓迎しないからであり、私もブーイングが起こらないうちにこの辺で終りにさせてもらう。

(continued from P. 5)
Words in brackets
—カッコの中の言葉について（Ｐ５から続く）

　In this phrasebook you see some phrases with additional words in brackets. The words in brackets are additional words that make the phrases sound more like "native-speakers'" polite Japanese. You can skip the words in brackets and still make sense, if the added words make the phrases too difficult for you to say. For example, "Good morning" in Japanese is "おはよう（ございます）／ ohayo (gozaimas)." This means that you can say either "ohayoo" or "ohayoo gozaimas." "Ohayoo" is a colloquial form of "ohayoo gozaimas" and is used by just as many Japanese when they don't need to be polite with their "seniors" and "superiors."

　本書中にあるカッコ内の言葉について説明します。カッコ内の言葉を入れると文章が長くなって読みにくい場合は、特に読まなくても結構です。読まなくとも意味は通じますが、読むことで"日本語のネイティブ"のような丁寧さの日本語になるはずです。一例を挙げると、日本語で「グッドモーニング」は「おはよう（ございます）」となりますが、「おはよう」でも「おはようございます」でも、伝わる意味は基本的に変わりません。年配者や先輩に気を遣わなくてもいい場面では、くだけた表現である「おはよう」を使う日本人も多くいます。

More on "Romanization" of Japanese sounds
—日本語の"ローマ字化"について

　The letter "n" usually becomes "m" before the letters "b", "m" and "p". For example, "shinbun (newspaper)" becomes "shimbun" and "nan-pun (how many minutes)" becomes "nam-pun."

　ｂ、ｍ、ｐの前に来たｎは、基本的にｍと綴られます。"newspaper"という意味の"shinbun"は、ｂの影響を受けて"shimbun"となります。"how many minutes"という意味の"nan-pun"も、ｐの影響を受けて"nam-pun"となります。

Section 3
第3部

English-Japanese Glossary of Additional Vocabulary Words

英語→日本語 単語集

This English-Japanese glossary features over 2000 everyday words to complement the "POINT-AND-SPEAK" conversation pages.

第3部の単語集には、指さしシートには収録できなかった日常会話用語彙を2000以上も厳選して収録しました。

A

English	日本語	Romaji
abacus	そろばん	soroban
abdominal muscle	腹筋	fukkin
above	上	u'e
accommodation	宿泊設備	shukuhaku setsubi
accountant	会計士	kaikee-shi
across the street	通りの向こう	toori no mukoo
act (perform)	演技する	engi-suru
actor	俳優	hai-yuu
actress	女優	jo-yuu
add	足す	tasu
adjective	形容詞	keeyoo-shi
adjust	調整する	choosee-suru
admission	入場料	nyuujoo-ryoo
adult	大人	otona
advantage	利点	riten
adventure	冒険	booken
adverb	副詞	fuku-shi
advertisement	広告	kookoku
advice	アドバイス	adobaisu
aerobics	エアロビクス	e'aro-bikusu
afraid	こわい	kowai
after school	放課後	hooka-go
age	年齢	nenree
age (period in history)	時代	jidai
agonize	苦しむ	kurushimu
agree	賛成する	sansee-suru
AIDS	エイズ	eizu
air	空気	kuuki
airplane	飛行機	hikooki
airport	空港	kuukoo
album	アルバム	arubamu
alfalfa	アルファルファ	aru-farufa
alien (from outer space)	宇宙人	uchuu-jin
alien (non-Japanese)	外国人	gaikoku-jin
alien registration	外国人登録	gaikoku-jin tooroku
alive	生きてる	ikiteru
almond	アーモンド	aamondo
alone	ひとりで	hitori de
altitude	高度	koodo
altitude sickness	高山病	koozan-byoo
aluminum	アルミ	arumi
always	いつも	itsumo
amateur	アマチュア	ama-chu'a
American football	アメフト	ame-futo
amplifier	アンプ	ampu
amusement park	遊園地	yuu'enchi
amusing	愉快	yukai
angry	怒ってる	okkotteru
"angular" script (of Japanese)	カタカナ	kata-kana
animal	動物	doobutsu
anniversary	記念日	kinem-bi
announcer	アナウンサー	ana'unsaa
ant	アリ	ari
antenna	アンテナ	antena
antibiotics	抗生物質	koosee-busshitsu
apartment	アパート	apaato
appearance	外見	gaiken
appointment	アポ	apo
appropriate	適切	tekisetsu
apron	エプロン	epuron
archery (Japanese-style)	弓道	kyuu-doo
architecture	建築	kenchiku
area	地域	chiiki
area code	市外局番	shigai-kyokuban
aroma therapy	アロマテラピー	aroma-terapii
arrival	到着	toochaku
arrogant	横柄	oohee
art museum	美術館	bijutsu-kan
arthritis	関節炎	kansetsu-en
article (grammar)	冠詞	kan-shi
article (newspaper)	記事	kiji
artist	芸術家	geejutsu-ka
ask (a question)	たずねる	tazuneru
assailant	加害者	kagai-sha
assistant	助手	joshu
assistant professor	助教授	jo-kyooju
astigmatism	乱視	ranshi
astrology	占星術	sensee-jutsu
astronomy	天文学	tem'mon-gaku
atomic bomb	原爆	gembaku
attack	攻撃	koogeki
autograph	サイン	sain
automatic	自動	jidoo
automobile	自動車	jidoo-sha
average	平均的	heekin-teki
avocado	アボカド	abokado
awesome	すごい	sugoi
awkward	ぎこちない	gikochi-nai

B

English	日本語	Romaji
baby (infant)	赤ちゃん	aka-chan
back	後ろ	ushiro
backstroke	背泳ぎ	se'oyogi
backpack	リュック	ryukku
bad	悪い	warui
bad luck	悪運	aku'un
bag (paper or prastic)	袋	fukuro
bag (handbag, etc.)	かばん	kaban
baggage claim area	手荷物受取所	tenimotsu uketori-jo
baggage locker	ロッカー	rokkaa

104

English	Japanese	Romaji
bait	餌	esa
ballet	バレエ	baree
balloon	風船	fuusen
ballpark	野球場	yakyuu-joo
bamboo	竹	take
bamboo sword	竹刀	shinai
ban (to prohibit)	禁止	kinshi
banana	バナナ	banana
bandage	包帯	hootai
bangs	前髪	ma'e-gami
bar	酒場	sakaba
barbaric	野蛮	yaban
barbecue	バーベキュー	baabekyuu
barf	ゲロ	gero
bargain sale	売り出し	uri-dashi
bartender	バーテン	baaten
baseball	野球	yakyuu
basement	地下	chika
basin (river basin)	盆地	bonchi
basketball	バスケ	basuke
bass guitar	ベース	beesu
bath	風呂	furo
beach	海岸	kaigan
beach volleyball	ビーチバレー	biichi-baree
bear (animal)	熊	kuma
beard	顎鬚	ago-hige
beetle	甲虫	koochuu
belly button	へそ	heso
belt	ベルト	beruto
bench	ベンチ	benchi
betting	賭け事	kake-goto
bib (for babies)	よだれかけ	yodare-kake
bicycle	自転車	jitensha
big	大きい	ookii
bikini	ビキニ	bikini
bill (paper money)	紙幣	shihee
bisexual	両刀	ryootoo
black pepper	黒コショー	kuro-koshoo
blanket	毛布	moofu
blood	血	chi
blowfish	フグ	fugu
blush (cosmetics)	頬紅	hoo-beni
board	板	ita
boat	ボート	booto
body boarding	ボディボード	bodii-boodo
body building	ボディービル	bodii-biru
body fat	体脂肪	tai-shiboo
body odor	体臭	tai-shuu
bog	沼	numa
book (publication)	本	hon
boots	ブーツ	buutsu
boring	つまらない	tsumara-nai
born	生まれる	umareru
borrow	借りる	kariru
botanical garden	植物園	shokubutsu-en
bottle	瓶	bin
bouquet	花束	hana-taba
bowling	ボーリング	booringu
box office	プレイガイド	purei-gaido
boxing	ボクシング	boku-shingu
boy	男の子	otoko-no-ko
bracelet	ブレスレット	buresu-retto
braid (of hair)	おさげ	osage
Braille	点字	tenji
brakes	ブレーキ	bureeki
breast stroke	平泳ぎ	hira-oyogi
breath	息	iki
breath freshener	マウスペット	ma'usu-petto
bride	新婦	shimpu
bridegroom	新郎	shinroo
bridge	橋	hashi
bright	明るい	akarui
bronze	銅	doo
broom	ほうき	hooki
broth	汁	shiru
brunch	ブランチ	buranchi
brush	ブラシ	burashi
brush (painting)	筆	fude
Buddhism	仏教	bukkyoo
Buddhist monk	お坊さん	o-boo-san
budgerigar	インコ	inko
budget	予算	yosan
bug	虫	mushi
building	建物	tatemono
bum around	ブラブラする	burabura-suru
bus driver	バスの運転手	basu no unten-shu
business	商売	shoobai
business man	ビジネスマン	bijinesu-man
business woman	ビジネスウーマン	bijinesu-uuman
but	しかし	shikashi
butterfly (insect)	蝶	choo
butterfly stroke	バタフライ	bata-furai
button	ボタン	botan
buy	買う	ka'u
by ~self	自分で	jibun de

C

English	Japanese	Romaji
Cabinet (political body)	内閣	naikaku
cable car	ロープウェイ	roopuu'wei
cable TV	ケーブルテレビ	keeburu-terebi
cake	ケーキ	keeki
calcium	カルシウム	karushi'umu

English	Japanese	Romaji
calculate	計算する	keesan-suru
calendar	カレンダー	karendaa
calm (composed)	落ち着いた	ochi-tsuita
calorie	カロリー	karorii
camping	キャンプ	kyampu
campus	キャンパス	kyampasu
can (container)	缶	kan
candle	ろうそく	roosoku
canoe	カヌー	kanuu
capital (city)	首都	shuto
captain	キャプテン	kyaputen
car	車	kuruma
car navigation	カーナビ	kaa-nabi
caramel	キャラメル	kyara-meru
carbohydrate	炭水化物	tansui-kabutsu
cardboard	段ボール	dam-booru
cardigan	カーデガン	kaadegan
carotene	カロチン	karochin
carpenter	大工	daiku
carpet	絨毯	juutan
carry	運ぶ	hakobu
carry-on luggage	持ち込み手荷物	mochikomi-tenimotsu
cashew nut	カシューナッツ	kashuu-nattsu
castanets	カスタネット	kasuta-netto
castle	城	shiro
cat	猫	neko
cat nap	昼寝	hiru-ne
catch	捕る	toru
caterpillar	イモムシ	imo-mushi
cattle	牛	ushi
caution	注意	chuu'i
ceiling	天井	tenjoo
celery	セロリ	serori
cell battery	セル電池	seru-denchi
center	中心	chuushin
centigrade	摂氏	sesshi
centimeter	センチ	senchi
central	中心部の	chuushim-bu no
century	世紀	seeki
chair	イス	isu
change	変える	ka'eru
channel	チャンネル	chan'neru
chap (splitting of the skin)	ひび	hibi
character	人格	jinkaku
cheap	安い	yasui
check (written order for payment)	小切手	kogitte
check ~ out	チェックする	chekku-suru
cheerful	陽気	yooki
chef	シェフ	shefu
chef (of a Japanese restaurant)	板前	itama'e
cherry tree/blossoms	桜	sakura
chestnut	栗	kuri
childish	子供っぽい	kodomo-ppoi
child seat	チャイルドシート	chairudo-shiito
Chinese character	漢字	kanji
Chinese lantern (plant)	ほおずき	hoozuki
choreographer	振り付け師	furitsuke-shi
Christianity	キリスト教	kirisuto-kyoo
chrysanthemum	菊	kiku
cicada	セミ	semi
cigarette	タバコ	tabaco
citizenship	市民権	shimin-ken
city water	水道水	suidoo-sui
classified ads	分類広告	bunrui-kookoku
clean	きれい	kiree
cleaner	清掃員	seesoo-in
cleaning	クリーニング	kuriiningu
cleanly	きれい好き	kiree-zuki
clear (easy to understand)	ハッキリした	hakkiri-shita
clever	賢い	kashikoi
cliff	崖	gake
clock	置き時計	oki-dokee
close (shut)	閉じる	tojiru
clothes	服	fuku
cloud	雲	kumo
cockroach	ゴキブリ	gokiburi
coin	硬貨	kooka
cold	冷たい	tsumetai
collapse	倒れる	ta'oreru
collar	襟	eri
collision	衝突	shoototsu
cologne	コロン	koron
color	色	iro
come	来る	kuru
comet	彗星	suisee
comical	おもしろい	omoshiroi
commemoration	記念	kinen
commercial	商業的	shoogyoo-teki
commission	手数料	tesuu-ryoo
commute (to work)	通勤	tsuukin
commuter's pass	定期券	teeki-ken
compare	比べる	kuraberu
competition	競争	kyoosoo
complaint	文句	monku
complicated	複雑	fukuzatsu
compromise	妥協	dakyoo
conductor	車掌	shashoo
confrontation	対立	tairitsu
Confucianism	儒教	jukyoo
congratulate	祝う	iwa'u
conjunction (grammar)	接続詞	setsuzoku-shi
consciousness	意識	ishiki

English	日本語	Romaji
constitution (law)	憲法	kempoo
consulate	領事館	ryooji-kan
contact lens	コンタクトレンズ	kontakuto-renzu
contract	契約	keeyaku
convenient	便利	benri
cook (food)	料理する	ryoori-suru
cook (someone who cooks)	コック	kokku
cooperate	協力する	kyooryoku-suru
coordinator	コーディネーター	koodi-neetaa
coral	サンゴ	sango
corkscrew	コルク抜き	koruku-nuki
corn	トウモロコシ	too-morokoshi
corporal punishment	体罰	taibatsu
corridor	廊下	rooka
count	数える	kazo'eru
country	国	kuni
countryside	田舎	inaka
courage	勇気	yuuki
cover charge	カバー	kabaa
cow	雌牛	meushi
crawl (swimming)	クロール	kurooru
cream puff	シュークリーム	shuu-kuriimu
crisis	危機	kiki
criticize	批判する	hihan-suru
crocodile / alligator	ワニ	wani
croissant	クロワッサン	kurowassan
crow	カラス	karasu
crowded	混んでる	konderu
cry	泣く	naku
cultural heritage	文化遺産	bunka-isan
culture	文化	bunka
cunning	ズル賢い	zuru-gashikoi
curriculum	カリキュラム	kari-kyuram
cutter	カッター	kattaa
cycling	サイクリング	saiku-ringu
cymbals	シンバル	shim-baru

D

English	日本語	Romaji
dam	ダム	damu
damage	損害	songai
Damn!	チクショー！	chiku-shoo
dance	踊る	odoru
dancer	ダンサー	dansaa
dandelion	タンポポ	tampopo
danger	危険	kiken
Danish (pastry)	デニッシュ	denisshu
dark	暗い	kurai
date (day of the month)	日にち	hi-nichi
date (go out on a date)	デート	deeto
date of birth	生年月日	seenen-gappi
day	日	hi
day-care center	保育所	hoiku-jo
dead	死んだ	shinda
dean	学長	gaku-choo
debt	借金	shakkin
decide	決める	kimeru
decimal (math)	小数	shoo-suu
declaration form	申告用紙	shinkoku-yooshi
decline	遠慮する	enryo-suru
deficit	赤字	aka-ji
degree (academic title)	学位	gakui
delivery	配達	haitatsu
demotion	降格	kookaku
dental floss	糸ようじ	ito-yoogi
deny	否定する	hitee-suru
departure	出発	shuppatsu
depressed	落ち込んだ	ochikonda
designer	デザイナー	dezainaa
desk	机	tsuku'e
diaper	おむつ	omutsu
diary	日記	nikki
dictionary	辞書	jisho
die	死ぬ	shinu
diesel	軽油	keeyu
diet (go on a diet)	ダイエット	dai'etto
Diet (Parliament)	国会	kokkai
Diet building	国会議事堂	kokkai gijidoo
difficult	難しい	muzuka-shii
dimple	えくぼ	ekubo
dining car	食堂車	shokudoo-sha
direction	方向	hookoo
director	ディレクター	direkutaa
dirty	汚い	kitanai
disabled	障害者	shoogai-sha
disagree	反対する	hantai-suru
discount	割引	waribiki
dislike	嫌い	kirai
dislocated	脱臼	dakkyuu
display (exhibition)	展示	tenji
disqualify	失格	shikkaku
dissatisfaction	不満	fuman
district	地方	chihoo
divide (math)	割る	waru
diving	ダイビング	daibingu
dog paddle	犬かき	inu-kaki
dolphin	イルカ	iruka
domestic violence	家庭内暴力	katee-nai booryoku
Don't touch me!	さわるな！	sawaru-na
donut	ドーナツ	doonatsu
door	扉	tobira
downtown	繁華街	hanka-gai
dragonfly	トンボ	tombo

English	Japanese	Romaji
drama	ドラマ	dorama
draw (a picture)	描く	kaku
dream	夢	yume
dressing (for salads)	ドレッシング	doresshingu
drink	飲む	nomu
drinker (drinks alcohol)	飲める	nomeru
driver's license	運転免許	unten-menkyo
driver's seat	運転席	unten-seki
Drop dead!	死ね！	shine
drugs	薬	kusuri
illegal drugs	麻薬	mayaku
drums	ドラム、太鼓	doramu, taiko
dry	乾燥した	kansoo-shita
dry cleaning	ドライクリーニング	dorai kuriiningu
duel	決闘	kettoo
dumbfounded	呆れた	akireta
duration	期間	kikan
duty-free shop	免税店	menzee-ten

E

English	Japanese	Romaji
eagle	ワシ	washi
earlobe	耳たぶ	mimi-tabu
early	早い	hayai
earrings	イアリング	i'a-ringu
earth (planet)	地球	chikyuu
eat	食べる	taberu
ecology	エコロジー	ekorojii
economy	経済	keezai
editing	編集	henshuu
editor	編集者	henshuu-sha
election	選挙	senkyo
electric appliance	電化製品	denka-seehin
electric outlet	コンセント	konsento
electric power	電力	den-ryoku
electrical engineering	電気工学	denki-koogaku
electrician	電気技師	denki-gishi
electricity	電気	denki
elephant	象	zoo
elevator	エレベーター	ere-beetaa
embarrassed	恥ずかしい	hazuka-shii
embarrassing	恥ずかしい	hazuka-shii
embassy	大使館	taishi-kan
emergency	非常事態	hijoo-jitai
emergency exit	非常口	hijoo-guchi
emotion	感情	kanjoo
emotional	感情的	kanjoo-teki
encyclopedia	百科辞典	hyakka-jiten
engineer	エンジニア	enjini'a
enjoy	楽しむ	tanoshimu
enlarge	拡大する	kakudai-suru
Enough is enough!	いい加減にしろ！	ii-kagen ni shiro

English	Japanese	Romaji
enter	入る	hairu
enthusiastic	熱心	nesshin
entrance	入り口	iriguchi
entrepreneur	起業家	kigyoo-ka
environment	環境	kankyoo
equality	平等	byoodoo
eraser	消しゴム	keshi-gomu
escalator	エスカレーター	esuka-reetaa
estimate (probable cost)	見積り	mitsumori
ethnic	エスニック	esu-nikku
event	イベント	ibento
exam / test	試験	shiken
exchange	交換	kookan
excitement	興奮	koofun
excrement	大便	dai-ben
excuse	言い訳	iiwake
exercise	体操	taisoo
exit	出口	deguchi
expectation	期待	kitai
expenditure	支出	shishutsu
expensive	高い	takai
experience	経験	keeken
expert	エキスパート	ekisu-paato
explanation	説明	setsu-mee
explore	探検する	tanken-suru
export	輸出	yushutsu
extra	余分	yobun
extra curricular activity	課外活動	kagai katsudoo
eyebrow	眉毛	mayu-ge
eyedrops	目薬	me-gusuri
eyelash	睫毛	matsuge

F

English	Japanese	Romaji
fabric	織物	orimono
facet	蛇口	jaguchi
facial treatment	フェイシャル	feisharu
factory	工場	koojoo
factory outlet	アウトレット	a'uto-retto
factory worker	工場勤め	koojoo-zutome
Fahrenheit	華氏	kashi
failure	失敗	shippai
fairy tale	おとぎ話	otogi-banashi
fake	ニセモノ	nisemono
false tooth	入れ歯	ireba
family name	名字	myooji
famous	有名	yuumee
fan (enthusiast, supporter)	ファン	fan
farmer	農業従事者	noogyoo juuji-sha
far-sighted	遠視	enshi
fart	おなら	onara
fast	早く	hayaku

English	Japanese	Romaji
fast food	ファストフード	faasuto-fuudo
fat (person)	デブ	debu
fat (plumpness, obesity)	ぜい肉	zeeniku
favor(kind act)	お願い	onegai
favorite	お気に入り	okini'iri
feast	ごちそう	gochisoo
feeling	感覚	kankaku
feelings	感情	kanjoo
fence	柵	saku
ferry	フェリー	ferii
fiancé / fiancée	フィアンセ	fi'anse
fiber	繊維	sen'i
field	畑	hatake
find	見つける	mitsukeru
fine (penalty)	罰金	bakkin
fingernail	爪	tsume
fire engine	消防自動車	shooboo jidoo-sha
fire escape	非常階段	hijoo-kaidan
fire station	消防署	shooboo-sho
first name	名前	nama'e
first sex	初体験	hatsu-taiken
fish market	魚市場	u'o-ichiba
fishery	漁業	gyogyoo
fishing in the river	川釣り	kawa-zuri
fishing in the sea	海釣り	umi-zuri
fishing rod	竿	sa'o
fitness center	フィットネスセンター	fitto-nesu sentaa
fitting room	試着室	shichaku-shitsu
flavor	味	aji
flexible	柔軟	juunan
floor	床	yuka
floppy disk	フロッピー	furoppii
flower	花	hana
fly	飛ぶ	tobu
fly fishing	フライ釣り	furai-zuri
focus (of a camera)	ピント	pinto
fold	折る	oru
food	食べ物	tabemono
food stand/stall	屋台	yatai
fool	馬鹿	baka
foot reflexology	足裏マッサージ	ashi-ura massaaji
football	フットボール	futto-booru
footbridge	歩道橋	hodoo-kyoo
foreign language	外国語	gaikoku-go
foreign trade	貿易	boo'eki
foreigner (non-Japanese)	外国人、外人	gaikoku-jin, gaijin
forest	森	mori
fox	キツネ	kitsune
fraction (math)	分数	bunsuu
fragrant	かぐわしい	kaguwashii
free (of charge)	無料	muryoo
free time	自由時間	jiyuu-jikan
freedom	自由	jiyuu
freelance	フリー	furii
freshwater	淡水	tansui
friendship	友情	yuujoo
Frisbee	フリスビー	furisubii
frog	カエル	ka'eru
front	前	ma'e
frost	霜	shimo
frost bite	しもやけ	shimo-yake
frustrated	悔しい	kuyashii
frying pan	フライパン	furai-pan
fuck(sex)	やる	yaru
Fuck!	クソッタレ！	kussottare
fun	楽しい	tanoshii
funeral	葬式	soo-shiki
funky	ファンキー	fankii
furniture	家具	kagu
future	未来	mirai

G

English	Japanese	Romaji
gallery	ギャラリー	gyararii
game	試合	shi'ai
garbage	ゴミ	gomi
flammable	燃えるゴミ	mo'eru gomi
inflammable	燃えないゴミ	mo'e-nai gomi
garbage bin	ゴミ箱	gomi-bako
garden	庭	niwa
gardening	ガーデニング	gaade-ningu
gas station	ガソリンスタンド	gasorin sutando
gasoline	ガソリン	gasorin
gay (homosexual)	ゲイ	gei
gear	ギア	gi'a
genetic engineering	遺伝子工学	idenshi-koogaku
genius	天才	tensai
gesture	身振り	miburi
Get away!	どけ！	doke
Get lost!	あっち行け！	acchi ike
get off (a bus, train, etc.)	乗る	noru
get on (a bus, train, etc.)	降りる	oriru
get up	起きる	okiru
gift-wrap	包装する	hoosoo-suru
gin	ジン	jin
giraffe	キリン	kirin
girl	女の子	on'na-no-ko
give	あげる	ageru
glass (substance)	ガラス	garasu
glasses (eyeglasses)	眼鏡	megane
gloves	手袋	tebukuro
go	行く	iku
god	神	kami

English	日本語	Romaji
goddess	女神	megami
golf	ゴルフ	gorufu
gonorrh(o)ea	梅毒	baidoku
good	良い	ii
Good bye and good riddance!..	せいせいした！	seesee shita
good luck	幸運	koo'un
good time (fun)	楽しい	tanoshii
good-for-nothing	ロクでなし	rokude-nashi
gourmet	グルメ	gurume
government	政府	seefu
graduation	卒業	sotsugyoo
gram	グラム	guramu
grammar	文法	bumpoo
grass	草	kusa
grasshopper	バッタ	batta
grave (place of burial)	墓	haka
gray hair	白髪	shiraga
ground	地面	jimen
group	集団	shuudan
group photo	集合写真	shuugoo-shashin
guide (tour guide)	ガイド	gaido
guilty	後ろめたい	ushiro-metai
guitar	ギター	gitaa
gum(teeth)	歯茎	haguki
guts	根性	konjoo
gym	ジム	jimu
gymnasium	体育館	tai'iku-kan

H

English	日本語	Romaji
hail	ひょう	hyoo
hail (pellets of ice)	あられ	arare
hair loss	抜け毛	nuke-ge
hair removal	脱毛	datsu-moo
hairstyle	髪型	kami-gata
half-price	半額	han-gaku
hammer	金槌	kanazuchi
handbag	ハンドバッグ	hando-baggu
handball	ハンドボール	hando-booru
happy	嬉しい	ureshii
hard time (have a)	大変	taihen
harmonica	ハーモニカ	haamonika
hate	憎む	nikumu
hawk	タカ	taka
heal	癒す	iyasu
health	健康	kenkoo
health food	健康食品	kenkoo-shokuhin
hear	聞く	kiku
heart (seat of feelings)	心	kokoro
heat	熱	netsu
heating	暖房	damboo
heavy	重い	omoi
height	高さ	takasa
helicopter	ヘリコプター	heri-koputaa
help (offer assistance)	手伝う	tetsuda'u
herb	薬草	yakusoo
heritage	遺産	isan
herpes	ヘルペス	heru-pesu
Hey!	ちょっと	chotto
hiccup	しゃっくり	shakkuri
high	高い	takai
high-calorie	高カロリー	koo-karorii
highlight	見所	midokoro
highlight marker	蛍光ペン	keekoo-pen
highrise building	高層ビル	koosoo-biru
highway	高速道路	koosoku-dooro
hiking	ハイキング	haikingu
Hindu	ヒンズー教	hinzuu-kyoo
historic	歴史的	rekishi-teki
hitch-hike	ヒッチハイク	hicchi-haiku
hole	穴	ana
home	家	i'e
come (go) home	帰宅	kitaku
homecoming	帰省	kisee
homeless	ホームレス	hoomu-resu
homeroom teacher	担任	tan'nin
homework	宿題	shukudai
honesty	正直	shoojiki
hook (fishing)	針	hari
horn (of a car)	警笛	keeteki
hostess	ホステス	hosutesu
hostility	敵意	teki'i
hot	熱い	atsui
hot cake	ホットケーキ	hotto-keeki
hot spring	温泉	onsen
House of Councilors	参議院	sangi'in
House of Representatives	衆議院	shuugi'in
housing complex	団地	danchi
how	どのように	dono-yooni
human rights	人権	jinken
humidity	湿度	shitsudo
hungry	空腹	kuufuku
hunting	狩り	kari
hygiene	衛生	eesee

I

English	日本語	Romaji
I knew it	やっぱりね	yappari-ne
I see	なるほど	naruhodo
idea	アイディア	aide'a
Idiot!	バカ！	baka
ignore	無視する	mushi-suru
illegal	違法	ihoo

English	Japanese	Romaji
illumination	照明	shoomee
immigrant	移民	imin
import	輸入	yu'nyuu
important	大切	taisetsu
impractical	非実用的	hi-jitsuyoo-teki
improvement	向上	koojoo
in the past	以前	izen
incense	線香	senkoo
include	含む	fukumu
income	収入	shuu'nyuu
incomplete	不完全	fukanzen
inconvenient	不便	fuben
industry	業界、工業	gyookai, koogyoo
infamous	悪名高い	aku'myoo takai
inflammation	炎症	enshoo
influence	影響	eekyoo
information	情報	joohoo
injury	怪我	kega
inquiry	問い合わせ	toi-awase
insect	昆虫	konchuu
insect repellent	虫除け	mushi-yoke
inside	内側	uchi-gawa
insomnia	不眠症	fumin-shoo
insurance policy	保険証書	hoken-shoosho
intelligence	知性	chisee
intensive	集中的	shuuchuu-teki
intention	意図	ito
international	国際的	kokusai-teki
international driver's license	国際免許	kokusai-menkyo
international-minded	国際派	kokusai-ha
interpreter	通訳	tsuuyaku
intervene	干渉	kanshoo
invent	発明する	hatsumee-suru
invoice	請求書	seekyuu-sho
iron	鉄	tetsu
irritable	怒りっぽい	okorippoi
Islam	イスラム教	isuramu-kyoo
island	島	shima
itch suppressant	かゆみ止め	kayumi-dome
itinerary	旅程	ryotee

J

English	Japanese	Romaji
jail	刑務所	keemusho
janitor	用務員	yoomu-in
Japanese (of Japan)	日本的	nihon-teki
Japanese music	邦楽	hoogaku
Japanese paper	和紙	washi
jealousy	嫉妬	shitto
jellyfish	クラゲ	kurage
jet lag	時差ボケ	jisa-boke
jewel	宝石	hooseki
jogging	ジョギング	jogingu
joke	冗談	joodan
Judaism	ユダヤ教	yudaya-kyoo
jump	跳ねる	haneru

K

English	Japanese	Romaji
keep (a pet)	飼う	ka'u
kerosene	灯油	tooyu
kettle	やかん	yakan
key	鍵	kagi
kick	蹴る	keru
kick-boxing	キックボクシング	kikku boku-shingu
kill	殺す	korosu
kiln (pottery)	窯	kama
kilogram	キロ (グラム)	kiro (guramu)
kilometer	キロ (メートル)	kiro (meetoru)
kind (sort, type)	種類	shurui
kindness	親切	shinsetsu
kiss	キス	kisu
kitchen	台所	daidokoro
kiwi	キウイ	ki'ui
knife	ナイフ	naifu
knitting	編物	amimono
know	知ってる	shitteru
knowledge	知識	chishiki

L

English	Japanese	Romaji
labor	労働	roodoo
labor union	労働組合	roodoo kumi'ai
ladder	梯子	hashigo
ladies' room	女子トイレ	joshi-toire
ladle	おたま	otama
lake	湖	mizu-umi
landscape	風景	fuukee
lantern	提灯	choochin
last name	名字	myooji
late	遅い	osoi
laugh	笑う	wara'u
laughter	笑い	warai
laundry (clothes to wash)	洗濯物	sentaku-mono
lawn	芝生	shibafu
leave school (before graduation)	中退	chuutai
left-handed	左利き	hidari-kiki
lend	貸す	kasu
length	長さ	nagasa
lesbian	レズ	rezu
lesson	授業	jugyoo
letter	手紙	tegami
liar	ウソつき	uso-tsuki
license	免許証	menkyo-shoo
lick	なめる	nameru

English	Japanese	Romaji
lid	蓋	futa
lie	嘘	uso
life (⇔death)	命	inochi
life (lifetime)	人生	jinsee
life (living)	生活	seekatsu
lifestyle	生活様式	seekatsu-yooshiki
light (illumination)	明かり	akari
lighter	ライター	raitaa
lightweight	軽い	karui
lily	ユリ	yuri
limousine	リムジン	rimujin
line up	並ぶ	narabu
linguistics	言語学	gengo-gaku
lion	ライオン	rai'on
lip	唇	kuchi-biru
lip balm / cream	リップクリーム	rippu kuriimu
lipstick	口紅	kuchi-beni
literature	文学	bungaku
lithium battery	リチウム電池	richi'umu denchi
live	生きる	ikiru
live music	ライブ	raibu
lizard	トカゲ	tokage
local	地元の	jimoto-no
local call	市内通話	shinai-tsuuwa
long	長い	nagai
long distance train	長距離列車	choo-kyori ressha
lot (decide by lot)	くじびき	kuji-biki
low	低い	hikui
low-calorie	低カロリー	tee-karoii
lower-class	低所得層	tee-shotoku-soo
lunatic	キチガイ	kichigai
lure fishing	ルアー釣り	ru'aa-zuri

M

English	Japanese	Romaji
magazine	雑誌	zasshi
maid	メイド	meedo
mailbox	郵便ポスト	yuubim-posuto
major (in a subject)	専攻	senkoo
make	つくる	tsukuru
marathon	マラソン	marason
marker	マーカー	maakaa
martial arts	格闘技	kakutoo-gi
mask (ornamental)	面	men
mask (surgical)	マスク	masuku
massage	マッサージ	massaaji
match (to make fire)	マッチ	macchi
match (competition)	試合	shi'ai
mature	大人	otona
maximum	最大	saidai
meal	食事	shokuji
mechanical	機械的	kikai-teki
medical science	医学	igaku
medical worker	医療関係者	iryoo kankee-sha
meeting	会議	kaigi
member	会員	kai'in
membership card	会員証	kai'in-shoo
memorize	暗記する	anki-suru
men's room	男子トイレ	danshi-toire
merchandise	商品	shoohin
messy	ゴチャゴチャした	gocha-gocha shita
metal	金属	kinzoku
meter (device)	メーター	meetaa
meter (length)	メートル	meetoru
microwave oven	電子レンジ	denshi-renji
mid summer	真夏	manatsu
mid winter	真冬	mafuyu
middle	真ん中	man'naka
middle age	中年	chuunen
middle-class	中流	chuu-ryuu
military worker	軍事関係者	gunji kankee-sha
millimeter	ミリ	miri
millionaire	億万長者	okuman-chooja
mind (center of thought)	心	kokoro
mind (faculty of thinking)	頭	atama
mini bar	ミニバー	mini-baa
minimum	最小	saishoo
mirror	鏡	kagami
mistake	ミス	misu
misunderstanding	誤解	gokai
mixed blood	混血	konketsu
model	モデル	moderu
modem	モデム	modemu
modem cable	モデムケーブル	modemu keeburu
modern	近代的	kindai-teki
mold / mildew	かび	kabi
money	金、お金	kane, okane
monorail	モノレール	mono-reeru
month	月	tsuki
moon	月	tsuki
moped	原付	gen-tsuki
morning glory (plant)	朝顔	asa-ga'o
moth	蛾	ga
mother tongue	母国語	bokoku-go
motorbike	バイク	baiku
mountain	山	yama
mountain climbing	山登り	yama-nobori
movie theater	映画館	eega-kan
moving (touching)	感動	kandoo
multiply (math)	かける	kakeru
muscle	筋肉	kin'niku
music	音楽	ongaku
country	カントリー	kantorii

English	日本語	Romaji
classical	クラシック	kura-shikku
folk	フォーク	fooku
funk	ファンク	fanku
heavy metal	ヘビメタ	hebi-meta
jazz	ジャズ	jazu
pop	ポップス	poppusu
rap	ラップ	rappu
reggae	レゲエ	regee
rock	ロック	rokku
musical instrument	楽器	gakki
musician	音楽家	ongaku-ka
mustache	口髭	kuchi-hige
myth	神話	shin'wa

N

English	日本語	Romaji
nail (piece of metal)	釘	kugi
nail polish	マニキュア	mani-kyu'a
nail polish remover	徐光液	jokoo-eki
narrow	狭い	semai
narrow-minded	心が狭い	kokoro ga semai
nation	国家	kokka
national anthem	国歌	kokka
national flag	国旗	kokki
national park	国立公園	kokuritsu-koo'en
nature	自然	shizen
near-sighted	近視	kinshi
necklace	ネックレス	nekku-resu
need	必要	hitsuyoo
needle	針	hari
neighborhood	近所	kinjo
neon	ネオン	ne'on
nephew	おい	oi
net	網	ami
news	ニュース	nyuusu
newspaper	新聞	shimbun
nickname	ニックネーム	nikku-neemu
niece	めい	mei
night club	ナイトクラブ	naito-kurabu
nightlife	夜遊び	yo'asobi
nightmare	悪夢	akumu
nipple	乳首	chikubi
no good	ダメ	dame
No…	ああ…	aa
noise	騒音	soo'on
noisy	うるさい	urusai
non-commercial	非商業的	hi-shoogyoo-teki
non-drinker	飲めない	nome-nai
northeast	北東	hoku-too
northwest	北西	hoku-see
notebook	ノート	nooto
noun	名詞	meeshi
now	今	ima
nuclear	核	kaku
nuisance	迷惑	meewaku
number	数	kazu
nursing care	介護	kaigo
nutrition	栄養	eeyoo
nympho	ヤリマ	yari-ma

O

English	日本語	Romaji
obligation	義務	gimu
observe (study)	観察する	kansatsu-suru
oddball	変人	henjin
odds-on favorite	本命	hom'mee
office	事務所	jimu-sho
office clerk	事務員	jimu-in
official	係員	kakari'in
official language	公用語	kooyoo-go
Oh!	ええ〜	ee
oil	油	abura
oil/petrol	石油	sekiyu
oil colors (coloring substance)	油絵の具	abura-enogu
oil colors (painting)	油絵	abura-e
oily	油っこい	abura-kkoi
old	古い	furui
old (for people)	年のいった	toshi-no-itta
old-fashioned	昔ながらの	mukashi-nagara no
one-day ticket	１日乗車券	ichi-nichi joosha-ken
one-way	片道	kata-michi
open	開く	hiraku
open-minded	心が広い	kokoro ga hiroi
operator	オペレーター	opereetaa
opinion	意見	iken
optimistic	楽観的	rakkan-teki
orange	オレンジ	orenji
organ	オルガン	orugan
outside	外側	soto-gawa
oven	オーブン	oobun
overdrink	飲み過ぎ	nomi-sugi
overeat	食べ過ぎ	tabe-sugi
oversleep	寝坊	neboo
overtime (work)	残業	zangyoo
ox	雄牛	oushi

P

English	日本語	Romaji
Pacific Ocean	太平洋	taihee-yoo
pacifier (for babies)	おしゃぶり	oshaburi
packaged tour	パック旅行	pakku-ryokoo
pain	痛み	itami
pain reducer	痛み止め	itami-dome
painter	画家	gaka
painting	絵画	kaiga
palmistry	手相	tesoo

English	Japanese	Romaji
pamphlet	パンフ	panfu
paper	紙	kami
parasol	日傘	higasa
parcel	小包	kozutsumi
park	公園	koo'en
parka	パーカ	paaka
parking	駐車	chuusha
parking lot	駐車場	chuusha-joo
parsley	パセリ	paseri
party	パーティー	paatii
pass (exams)	合格	gookaku
pass away (die)	亡くなる	nakunaru
pass out (faint)	失神	shisshin
passenger's seat	助手席	joshu-seki
passion	情熱	joonetsu
past	過去	kako
pastime	ヒマつぶし、趣味	hima-tsubushi, shumi
patient	我慢強い	gaman-zuyoi
patient (at hospitals)	患者	kanja
pawnshop	質屋	shichi-ya
peace	平和	heewa
peanut	ピーナッツ	piinattsu
pearl	真珠	shinju
pedicure	ペディキュア	pedi-kyu'a
pee (urine)	おしっこ	oshikko
pen case	筆箱	fude-bako
penalty	罰則	bassoku
pencil	鉛筆	empitsu
pencil sharpener	鉛筆けずり	empitsu-kezuri
peninsula	半島	hantoo
percent	パーセント	paasento
perfect	完璧	kampeki
persistent	しつこい	shitsukoi
personal	個人的	kojin-teki
personal organizer (notebook)	システム手帳	shisutemu techoo
personality	性格、個性	seekaku, kosee
persuade	説得する	settoku-suru
pessimistic	悲観的	hikan-teki
PET bottle	ペットボトル	petto-botoru
petrol / oil	石油	sekiyu
photographer	写真家	shashin-ka
physical strength	体力	tairyoku
piano	ピアノ	pi'ano
pickup service (for guests)	送迎	soogee
pierced earrings	ピアス	pi'asu
pig	豚	buta
pillar	柱	hashira
pilot	パイロット	pairotto
pimple	ニキビ	nikibi
piss	ションベン	shom-ben
place of birth	生まれた所	umareta-tokoro
plain (flat land)	平野	heeya
plan	計画	keekaku
planetarium	プラネタリウム	puraneta-ri'umu
plant (flowers & vegetables)	植物	shokubutsu
platform	ホーム	hoomu
play (music)	演奏する	ensoo-suru
play (sports)	する、やる	suru, yaru
pleasure boat	遊覧船	yuuran-sen
plastic	ビニール	biniiru
pliers	ペンチ	penchi
plum	梅	ume
plural (grammar)	複数形	fukusuu-kee
poem	詩	shi
poison	毒	doku
police station	警察署	keesatsu-sho
policewoman	婦人警官	fujin-keekan
political party	政党	seetoo
political science	政治科学	seeji-kagaku
politics	政治	seeji
polo shirt	ポロシャツ	poro-shatsu
pond	池	ike
ponytail	ポニーテール	ponii-teeru
popularity	人気	ninki
population	人口	jinkoo
porch	ポーチ	poochi
pornography	ポルノ	poruno
postage stamp	切手、郵便切手	kitte, yuubin-kitte
postal savings account	郵便貯金口座	yuubin-chokin-kooza
poster	ポスター	posutaa
postpostional particle	助詞	jo-shi
postwar	戦後	sengo
pottery	陶器	tooki
powder	粉	kona
powerful	力強い	chikara-zuyoi
practical	実用的	jitsuyoo-teki
prefecture	県	ken
prejudice	偏見	henken
premier (movie)	ロードショー	roodo-shoo
prepare	準備する	jumbi-suru
presbyopia	老眼	roogan
present (now)	現在	genzai
President (of a nation)	大統領	dai-tooryoo
prevent	防ぐ	fusegu
prewar	戦前	senzen
price	価格、値段	kakaku, nedan
prickly heat	あせも	asemo
priest	神父	shimpu
Prime Minister	首相	shushoo
principal (of a school)	校長	koochoo
private	プライベート	purai-beeto
private school	私立学校	shiritsu-gakkoo

English	Japanese	Romaji
pro wrestling	プロレス	puro-resu
problem	問題	mondai
producer	演出家	enshutsu-ka
professional	プロ	puro
professional athlete	プロスポーツ選手	puro-supootsu-senshu
professor	教授	kyooju
program (on TV)	番組	bangumi
promise	約束	yakusoku
promotion (advancement in rank)	昇進	shooshin
pronoun	代名詞	dai-mee-shi
proper noun	固有名詞	koyuu-mee-shi
prostitution	売春	bai-shun
protection	保護	hogo
protein	たんぱく質	tampaku-shitsu
public bath	銭湯	sentoo
public enemy	社会の敵	shakai no teki
public opinion	世論	seron, yoron
public restroom	公衆便所	kooshuu-benjo
public school	公立学校	kooritsu gakkoo
public telephone	公衆電話	kooshuu-den'wa
pudding	プリン	purin
pull	引く	hiku
punch (hit)	殴る	naguru
puppet	人形	ningyoo
puppy love	初恋	hatsu-koi
push	押す	osu
push-up (exercise for arms)	腕立て	ude-tate

Q

English	Japanese	Romaji
quality	品質	hin-shitsu
quarrel	口喧嘩	kuchi-genka
question	質問	shitsumon
quit	やめる	yameru

R

English	Japanese	Romaji
raccoon dog	タヌキ	tanuki
race	レース	reesu
race (ethnicity)	人種	jinshu
radio	ラジオ	raji'o
railroad tracks	線路	senro
rain	雨	ame
rainbow	虹	niji
rapids (of a river)	渓流	keeryuu
raw (food)	生	nama
ray (marine fish)	エイ	ei
read	読む	yomu
rear	後ろ	ushiro
reason	理由	riyuu
reason for living	生き甲斐	ikigai
reasonable	リーズナブル	riizu-naburu
receive	受け取る	uke-toru
receiver (telephone)	受話器	juwaki
recharge	充電	juuden
rechargeable battery	充電池	juu-denchi
recommend	すすめる	susumeru
record (musical medium)	レコード	rekoodo
record (set down for preservation)	記録する	kiroku-suru
red pepper	赤とうがらし	aka too-garashi
refills (for pens)	替芯	ka'e-shin
refund	返金	henkin
refuse	断る	kotowaru
registered mail	書留	kakitome
related	関係ある	kankee aru
relationship	関係	kankee
relative pronoun	関係代名詞	kankee-da'imee-shi
reliable	頼れる	tayoreru
religion	宗教	shuukyoo
religious	宗教的	shuukyoo-teki
remember	思い出す	omoi-dasu
remote control	リモコン	rimo-kon
renovation	改修	kaishuu
rent-a-car	レンタカー	renta-kaa
reputation	評判	hyooban
reserve	予約する	yoyaku-suru
reserved	予約済み	yoyaku-zumi
respect	尊敬	sonkee
retarded	知恵遅れ	chi'e-okure
retirement	引退	intai
return	返す	ka'esu
review (school work)	復習	fukushuu
ribbon	リボン	ribon
rice cooker	炊飯器	suihan-ki
rice paddy	田んぼ	tambo
ride	乗る	noru
right	正しい	tadashii
right (just claim)	権利	kenri
right-handed	右利き	migi-kiki
ring (sumo)	土俵	dohyoo
ring (worn on a finger)	指輪	yubi-wa
river	川	kawa
road	道路, 道	dooro, michi
road atlas	道路地図	dooro-chizu
rock (stone)	岩	iwa
role model	手本	tehon
rollerblading	ローラーブレード	rooraa-bureedo
rollerskating	ローラースケート	rooraa-sukeeto
roof	屋根	yane
rooftop	屋上	okujoo
rookie	新人	shin-jin
room maid	ルームメイド	ruumu meido
room number	部屋の番号	heya no bangoo
rose (flower)	バラ	bara
round trip	往復	oofuku

English	Japanese	Romaji
route map (of rail lines)	路線図	rosen-zu
rowboat	手漕ぎボート	tekogi-booto
ruby	ルビー	rubii
rugby football	ラグビー	ragubii
rum	ラム	ramu
run	走る	hashiru
running	ランニング	ran'ningu
"running" script (of Japanese)	ひらがな	hira-gana

S

English	Japanese	Romaji
sad	悲しい	kanashii
safe	安全	anzen
safety box	金庫	kinko
sailing	セイリング	seiringu
salesman	セールスマン	seerusu-man
saleswoman	セールスウーマン	seerusu-uuman
salt water	海水	kaisui
sand	砂	suna
sarcasm	皮肉	hiniku
satellite	衛星	eesee
save	救う	sukuu
savings account	普通口座	futsuu-kooza
saying (proverb)	ことわざ	kotowaza
scale (weighing device)	体重計	taijuu-kee
scallop	ホタテ貝	hotate-gai
scarecrow	案山子	kakashi
scary	こわい	kowai
schedule	予定	yotee
school	学校	gakkoo
school building	校舎	koosha
school year	学年	gakunen
science fiction	SF	esu-efu
score	点数	tensuu
screen (for windows)	網戸	amido
sculpture	彫刻	chookoku
sea	海	umi
Sea of Japan	日本海	nihon-kai
seafood	海産物	kaisan-butsu
seafood shop	魚屋	sakana-ya
search	探す	sagasu
season	季節	kisetsu
seasoning	調味料	choomi-ryoo
seat	席	seki
seaweed	海草	kaisoo
second-hand clothes	古着	furugi
secret	秘密	himitsu
see	見る	miru
Self Defense Forces	自衛隊	ji'ee-tai
self-centered	自己チュー	jiko-chuu
self-defense	正当防衛	seetoo-boo'ee
self-employed	自営業者	ji'eegyoo-sha
sell	売る	uru
send	送る	okuru
senility	老人ボケ	roojin-boke
sentence	文	bun
sentimental	感傷的	kanshoo-teki
service	サービス	saabisu
sesame	ゴマ	goma
set (a clock, timer, etc)	セットする	setto-suru
sewage	下水道	ge-suidoo
sewing	縫物	nuimono
sex	セックス	sekkusu
sex maniac	セックス中毒	sekkusu-chuudoku
sexless	セックスレス	sekkusu-resu
sexy	セクシー	sekushii
shape	形	katachi
share	分かち合う	wakachi-a'u
shaver	シェーバー	sheebaa
shaving cream	シェービングクリーム	sheebingu kuriimu
shelf	棚	tana
shellfish	貝	kai
shine	光る	hikaru
Shintoism	神道	shintoo
ship	船	fune
shit	ウンコ	unko
Shit!	クソ！	kuso
shock	ショック	shokku
shoelaces	靴ひも	kutsu-himo
shop clerk	商店勤務	shooten-kim'mu
shopkeeper	商店主	shooten-shu
shopping complex	ショッピングビル	shoppingu biru
short	短い	mijikai
shortest	最短	saitan
shorts	ショーツ	shootsu
shout	叫ぶ	sakebu
shovel	シャベル	shaberu
show	見せる	miseru
shrine	神社	jinja
Shut up!	黙れ	damare
sickle	鎌	kama
sideburns	もみ上げ	momi'age
signature	署名	shomee
simple	簡単	kantan
simple-minded	単純	tanjun
sincere	誠実	seejitsu
sing	歌う	uta'u
singer	歌手	kashu
singular (grammar)	単数形	tansuu-kee
sinker (fishing)	おもり	omori
sit	すわる	suwaru
sit-up	腹筋（運動）	fukkin(undoo)
sitcom	コメディードラマ	komedii dorama

English	Japanese	Romaji
size	大きさ	ookisa
skate	スケート	sukeeto
skate-boarding	スケボー	suke-boo
sketch book	スケッチブック	sukecchi-bukku
ski	スキー	sukii
skill	技術	gijutsu
skin	肌	hada
skinny	ヤセた	yaseta
sky	空	sora
sleep	寝る	neru
sleeper car	寝台車	shindai-sha
sleepy	眠い	nemui
slippers	スリッパ	surippa
slot machine	スロット	surotto
slow	遅い	osoi
slow (-witted)	トロイ	toroi
small change	小銭	kozeni
smelly	臭い	kusai
smile	笑顔	ega'o
sneakers	スニーカー	sunii-kaa
snow	雪	yuki
snow boarding	スノーボード	sunoo-boodo
social security	社会保障	shakai-hoshoo
society	社会	shakai
sociology	社会学	shakai-gaku
sofa	ソファー	sofaa
soil	土	tsuchi
soup	スープ	suupu
southeast	南東	nan-too
southwest	南西	nan-see
sparrow	スズメ	suzume
spatula (for cooking)	フライ返し	furai-ga'eshi
speak	話す	hanasu
specialist	専門家	sem'mon-ka
spider	クモ	kumo
spit	唾	tsuba
spoken language	口語	koo-go
spring break	春休み	haru-yasumi
squash (sport)	スカッシュ	sukasshu
squirrel	リス	risu
stage	舞台	butai
stain	しみ	shimi
stairs	階段	kaidan
stand	立つ	tatsu
standard lens	標準レンズ	hyoojun-renzu
staplers	ホッチキス	hocchi-kisu
star	星	hoshi
star sign	星座	seeza
station attendant	駅員	eki-in
station master	駅長	eki-choo
stationery	文房具	bumboogu
statue	像	zoo
steel	鋼鉄	koo-tetsu
steering wheel	ハンドル	handoru
sterilization	消毒	shoo-doku
steward	スチュワード	suchu-waado
stewardess	スチュワーデス	suchu-waadesu
sticker	シール	shiiru
stimulation	刺激	shigeki
stock	株	kabu
stock (of goods)	在庫	zaiko
stock raising	畜産	chikusan
stone	石	ishi
stop	止まる	tomaru
storm	嵐	arashi
strap (trains and buses)	吊り革	tsuri-kawa
street	通り、ストリート	toori, suto-riito
street tram	路面電車	romen-densha
strength	力	chikara
strike (hit)	叩く	tataku
strike (stopping of work)	スト	suto
strip teasing	ストリップ	suto-rippu
stroller (for babies)	ベビーカー	bebi-kaa
stubborn	ガンコ	ganko
study (examine)	研究する	kenkyuu-suru
study (schoolwork)	勉強する	benkyoo-suru
subject	科目	kamoku
subtract (math)	引く	hiku
success	成功	seekoo
suicide	自殺	jisatsu
suitcase	スーツケース	suutsu-keesu
suite	スイートルーム	su'iito ruumu
summer vacation	夏休み	natsu-yasumi
sun	太陽	taiyoo
sunbathe	日光浴	nikkoo-yoku
sunblock	日焼け止め	hiyake-dome
sunflower	ひまわり	himawari
sunglasses	サングラス	san-gurasu
sunrise	日の出	hinode
sunset	日の入り	hino'iri
sunstroke	日射病	nissha-byoo
suntan	日焼け	hiyake
Super Glue	瞬間接着剤	shunkan secchagu-zai
surfboard	サーフボード	saafu-boodo
surfing	サーフィン	saafin
surplus	黒字	kuro-ji
surprised	驚いた	odoroita
swallow (bird)	ツバメ	tsubame
sweat	汗	ase
swift	素早い	subayai
swim	泳ぐ	oyogu
swimming	水泳	sui'ee

English	Japanese	Romaji
swimming pool	プール	puuru
sword	刀	katana
symbol	象徴	shoochoo
system administrator	シスアド	shisu-ado

T

English	Japanese	Romaji
table	テーブル	teeburu
table tennis	卓球	takkyuu
tadpole	おたまじゃくし	otama-jakushi
take turns	順番に	jumban ni
talk	しゃべる	shaberu
talk show	トーク番組	tooku-bangumi
tanning salon	日焼けサロン	hiyake-saron
tariff	関税	kanzee
Tarot cards	タロット	tarotto
taste	味、味わう	aji, aji-wa'u
tattoo	刺青	irezumi
tax	税金	zeekin
taxi driver	タクシーの運転手	takushii no unten-shu
tea room	茶室	cha-shitsu
tea utensils	茶道具	cha-doogu
teacher	先生	sensee
teardrop	涙	namida
telegram	電報	dempoo
telephone pole	電柱	denchuu
telephoto lens	望遠レンズ	boo'en-renzu
television	テレビ	terebi
temperature	温度	ondo
temple	寺	tera
tennis	テニス	tenisu
tennis court	テニスコート	tenisu-kooto
term (of school year)	学期	gakki
textbook	教科書	kyooka-sho
theater	劇場	geki-joo
theft	盗難	toonan
thermometer	温度計	ondo-kee
thesis	論文	rom-bun
thick	厚い	atsui
thin	薄い	usui
thought	考え	kanga'e
thoughtful	考え深い	kanga'e-bukai
thread	糸	ito
throw	投げる	nageru
thunder	雷	kaminari
time difference	時差	jisa
tip (gratvity)	チップ	chippu
tire	タイヤ	taiya
tired (not interested)	飽きた	akita
tired (physical condition)	疲れた	tsuka-reta
toaster	トースター	toosutaa
together	いっしょに	issho ni
tomato	トマト	tomato
tool	道具	doogu
top (toy that spins)	こま	koma
topic (of conversation)	話題	wadai
topography	地形	chikee
tortoiseshell	べっこう	bekkoo
touch	触る	sawaru
tour conductor	ツアコン	tsu'a-kon
tour guide	ツアーガイド	tsu'aa gaido
tourist	ツーリスト	tsuu-risuto
tourist visa	観光ビザ	kankoo-biza
tow away	レッカー移動	rekkaa-idoo
tower	塔	too
town	町	machi
toy	おもちゃ	omocha
traditional	伝統的	dentoo-teki
traffic	交通	kootsuu
traffic sign	交通標識	kootsuu-hyooshiki
train	電車	densha
translation	翻訳	hon'yaku
translator	翻訳者	hon'yaku-sha
transportation	交通手段	kootsuu-shudan
travel	旅、旅行	tabi, ryokoo
travel agency	旅行代理店	ryokoo dairi-ten
travel insurance	旅行保険	ryokoo-hoken
tree	木	ki
trial (legal procedure)	裁判	saiban
trip	旅行	ryokoo
tripod	三脚	san-kyaku
truck	トラック	torakku
trumpet	トランペット	toram-petto
trunks	トランクス	torankusu
truth	真実	shin-jitsu
try	やってみる	yatte-miru
tulip	チューリップ	chuu-rippu
turkey	七面鳥	shichimen-choo
turn off (the light, etc.)	つける	tsukeru
turn on (the light, etc.)	消す	kesu
tweezers	毛抜き	ke-nuki
type	タイプ	taipu

U

English	Japanese	Romaji
unclear	ハッキリしない	hakkiri shinai
unconsciousness	無意識	mu-ikishi
underground	地下	chika
understanding	理解	rikai
unemployment insurance	失業保険	shitsugyoo-hoken
uniform	制服	seefuku
unisex	男女兼用	dan'jo-ken'yoo
universe (outer space)	宇宙	uchuu
unknown	無名	mu-mee

English	Japanese	Romaji
unnecessary	いらない	ira-nai
unpleasant	不愉快	fuyukai
unpopular	不人気	fu-ninki
unrelated	関係ない	kankee nai
unsympathetic	冷たい	tsumetai
unusual	他と違う	hoka to chiga'u
upbringing	しつけ	shitsuke
upper-class	上流階級	jooryuu kaikyuu
ups and downs	山あり谷あり	yama ari tani ari
urgent	緊急	kinkyuu
urine	小便	shoo-ben
use	使う	tsuka'u
useful	使える	tsuka'eru
useless	使えない	tsuka'e-nai

V

English	Japanese	Romaji
vacant	空いてる	suiteru
vacation	休暇	kyuuka
vacuum cleaner	電気掃除機	denki sooji-ki
valley	谷	tani
value	価値	kachi
variety show	バラエティー番組	bara'etii-bangumi
vase	花瓶	kabin
vegetarian	菜食主義	saishoku-shugi
venue	会場	ka'ijoo
verb	動詞	doo-shi
veteran (experienced)	ベテラン	beteran
vice-principal	教頭	kyootoo
vicinity	周辺	shuuhen
victim	被害者	higai-sha
video arcade	ゲームセンター	geemu-sentaa
village	村	mura
violation	反則	hansoku
virgin (boys)	童貞	dootee
virgin (girls)	処女	shojo
visa	ビザ	biza
visit	訪問	hoomon
vitamin	ビタミン	bitamin
vodka	ウォッカ	wokka
volleyball	バレーボール	baree-booru
volunteer	ボランティア	boranti'a
vomit	吐く	haku
Voodoo	ブーズー教	buuzuu-kyoo
vote	投票	toohyoo

W

English	Japanese	Romaji
wait	待つ	matsu
waiter	ウェイター	uwei-taa
waitress	ウェイトレス	uwei-toresu
wake up	目が覚める	me ga sameru
walk (for leisure)	散歩	sampo
wall	壁	kabe
wall clock	掛け時計	kake-dokee
walnut	クルミ	kurumi
war	戦争	sensoo
warning	警告	keekoku
wash	洗う	ara'u
washing clothes	洗濯	sentaku
watch (wristwatch)	腕時計	ude-dokee
water supply	水道	suidoo
watercolors (coloring substance)	水彩絵の具	suisai-enogu
watercolors (painting)	水彩画	suisai-ga
water-proof	防水	boosu'i
wave	波	nami
wealthy	裕福な	yuufuku-na
wear (clothes)	着る	kiru
wear (footwear)	履く	haku
web designer	ウェブデザイナー	webu dezainaa
wedding ceremony	結婚式	kekkon-shiki
week	週	shuu
weight-lifting	重量挙げ	juuryoo-age
welcome	歓迎	kangee
Well,…	え〜と	eeto
well-endowed (women)	ナイスバディ	naisu badii
well-known	有名な	yuumee-na
westernized	西洋的	seeyoo-teki
wet	濡れた	nureta
whale	クジラ	kujira
what	何	nani
wheat	小麦	komugi
when	いつ	itsu
where	どこ	doko
which	どれ	dore
who	だれ	dare
wide	広い	hiroi
wide-angle lens	広角レンズ	kookaku-renzu
wig	かつら	katsura
wildlife	野生動物	yasee-doobutsu
wind	風	kaze
window	窓	mado
window-shopping	ウィンドーショッピング	windoo shoppingu
winter break	冬休み	fuyu-yasumi
wisdom	知恵	chi'e
wish	願い	negai
wooden	木でできた	ki de dekita
wooden sword	木刀	boku-too
work	仕事	shigoto
work visa	ワーキングビザ	waakingu-biza
working holiday visa	ワーキングホリデービザ	waakingu-horidee-biza
world	世界	sekai
world heritage	世界遺産	sekai-isan
worry	心配	shimpai

119

worst	最悪	sai'aku
wrestling	レスリング	resu-ringu
write	書く	kaku
writer	物書き	mono-kaki
wrong	間違ってる	machi-gatteru
xylophone	木琴	mokkin

Y

yacht	ヨット	yotto
yawn	あくび	akubi
year	年	toshi
Yes!	よ〜し！	yooshi
young	若い	wakai
youth	青春	seeshun
youth hostel	ユースホステル	yuusu-hosuteru

Z

| zip code | 郵便番号 | yuubim-bangoo |
| zoo | 動物園 | doobutsu-en |

Section 4
第4部

Glossary of Japanese Holidays, Nations of the World, Etc.

日本の祝日、世界の国名など

This section features Japanese national holidays, tips on how to count in Japanese and how to pronounce the name of your country in Japanese.

第4部では、日本の祝日や日本語での数の数え方、さらには、読者のみなさんの国名を日本語でどう発音するかについてまとめました。

1 Nations of the World （世界の国々／sekai no kuni-guni）

Asia	アジア	aji'a
North America	北アメリカ	kita-america
South America	南アメリカ	minami-america
Europe	ヨーロッパ	yoo-roppa
Africa	アフリカ	afurika
Pacific Islands	太平洋諸島	taiheeyoo shotoo
Afghanistan	アフガニスタン	afugani-sutan
Albania	アルバニア	aruba-ni'a
Algeria	アルジェリア	aruje-ri'a
Andorra	アンドラ	andora
Angola	アンゴラ	angora
Antigua And Barbuda	アンティグア・バーブーダ	antigu'a baabuuda
Argentina	アルゼンチン	aruzen-chin
Armenia	アルメニア	arume-nia
Australia	オーストラリア	oosuto-rari'a
Austria	オーストリア	oosuto-ri'a
Azerbaijan	アゼルバイジャン	azeru-baijan
Bahamas (the)	バハマ	bahama
Bahrain	バーレーン	baareen
Bangladesh	バングラデシュ	bangura-deshu
Barbados	バルバドス	baru-badosu
Belarus	ベラルーシ	bera-ruushi
Belgium	ベルギー	berugii
Belize	ベリーズ	beriizu
Benin	ベナン	benan
Bhutan	ブータン	buutan
Bolivia	ボリビア	bori-bi'a
Bosnia and Herzegovina	ボスニア・ヘルツェゴビナ	bosuni'a herutse-gobina
Botswana	ボツワナ	botsu-wana
Brazil	ブラジル	burajiru
Brunei	ブルネイ	burunei
Bulgaria	ブルガリア	buru-gari'a
Burkina Faso	ブルキナファソ	burukina-faso
Burundi	ブルンジ	burunji
Cambodia	カンボジア	kam-boji'a
Cameroon	カメルーン	kameruun
Canada	カナダ	kanada
Cape Verde	カーボベルデ	kaabo-berude
Central African Republic	中央アフリカ共和国	chuu'oo afurika kyoowa-koku
Chad	チャド	chado
Chile	チリ	chiri
China	中国	chuugoku
Colombia	コロンビア	korom-bi'a
Comoros	コモロ	komoro
Congo (Democratic Republic of the)	コンゴ民主共和国	kongo minshu kyoowa-koku
Congo (Republic of the)	コンゴ共和国	kongo kyoowa-koku
Costa Rica	コスタリカ	kosuta-rica
Cote d'Ivoire	コートジボアール	kooto-jibo'aaru
Croatia	クロアチア	kuro-achi'a
Cuba	キューバ	kyuuba
Cyprus	キプロス	kipurosu
Czech Republic	チェコ共和国	cheko kyoowa-koku
Denmark	デンマーク	dem'maaku
Djibouti	ジブチ	jibuchi
Dominica	ドミニカ	dominika
Dominican Republic	ドミニカ共和国	dominika kyoowa-koku
Ecuador	エクアドル	eku'a-doru
Egypt	エジプト	ejiputo
El Salvador	エルサルバドル	eru saruba-doru
Equatorial Guinea	赤道ギニア	sekidoo gini'a
Eritrea	エリトリア	eri-toria
Estonia	エストニア	esu-toni'a
Ethiopia	エチオピア	echi-opi'a
Fiji	フィジー	fijii
Finland	フィンランド	fin-rando
France	フランス	furansu
Gabon	ガボン	gabon
Gambia (the)	ガンビア	gam-bi'a
Georgia	グルジア	guru-ji'a
Germany	ドイツ	doitsu
Ghana	ガーナ	gaana
Greece	ギリシャ	girisha
Grenada	グレナダ	gurenada
Guatemala	グアテマラ	gu'a-temara
Guinea	ギニア	gini'a
Guinea-Bissau	ギニアビサウ	gini'a-bisa'u
Guyana	ガイアナ	gai'ana
Haiti	ハイチ	haichi
Honduras	ホンジュラス	hon-jurasu
Hungary	ハンガリー	han-garii
Iceland	アイスランド	aisu-rando
India	インド	indo
Indonesia	インドネシア	indo-nesi'a
Iran	イラン	iran
Iraq	イラク	iraku
Ireland	アイルランド	airu-rando
Israel	イスラエル	isu-ra'eru
Italy	イタリア	itari'a
Jamaica	ジャマイカ	jamaika
Japan	日本	nihon, nippon
Jordan	ヨルダン	yorudan
Kazakhstan	カザフスタン	kazafu-stan
Kenya	ケニア	keni'a

Kiribati	キリバス	kiribasu		Portugal	ポルトガル	poru-togaru
Kuwait	クウェート	kuweeto		Qatar	カタール	kataaru
Kyrgyzstan	キルギス	kirugisu		Republic of Kosovo	コソボ	kosobo
Laos	ラオス	ra'osu		Romania	ルーマニア	ruu-mani'a
Latvia	ラトビア	rato-bi'a		Russia	ロシア	roshi'a
Lebanon	レバノン	rebanon		Rwanda	ルワンダ	ruwanda
Lesotho	レソト	resoto		St. Kitts And Nevis	セントクリストファー・ネイビス	sento kurisutofaa neibisu
Liberia	リベリア	ribe-ri'a				
Libya	リビア	ribi'a		St. Lucia	セントルシア	sento rushi'a
Liechtenstein	リヒテンシュタイン	rihiten-shutain		St. Vincent and the Grenadines	セントビンセント・グレナディーン諸島	sento bin-sento gurena-diin shotoo
Lithuania	リトアニア	rito-ani'a				
Luxembourg	ルクセンブルク	rukusen-buruku		Samoa	サモア	samo'a
Macedonia	マケドニア	make-doni'a		San Marino	サンマリノ	san-marino
Madagascar	マダガスカル	mada-gasukaru		Sao Tome and Principe	サントメ・プリンシペ	san-tome purin-shipe
Malawi	マラウイ	marawii				
Malaysia	マレーシア	maree-shi'a		Saudi Arabia	サウジアラビア	sa'uji arabi'a
Maldives	モルジブ	morujibu		Senegal	セネガル	senegaru
Mali	マリ	mari		Serbia	セルビア	serubi'a
Malta	マルタ共和国	maruta kyoowa-koku		Seychelles	セーシェル	seesheru
Marshall Islands	マーシャル諸島	maasharu shotoo		Sierra Leone	シェラレオネ	shera-re'one
Mauritania	モーリタニア	moori-tani'a		Singapore	シンガポール	shinga-pooru
Mauritius	モーリシャス	moo-rishasu		Slovakia	スロバキア	suro-baki'a
Mexico	メキシコ	mekishiko		Slovenia	スロベニア	suro-beni'a
Micronesia	ミクロネシア	mikuro-neshi'a		Solomon Islands	ソロモン諸島	soromon shotoo
Moldova	モルドバ	morudoba		Somalia	ソマリア	soma-ri'a
Monaco	モナコ	monako		South Africa	南アフリカ	minami afurika
Mongolia	モンゴル	mongoru		South Korea	韓国	kankoku
Montenegro	モンテネグロ	monteneguro		Spain	スペイン	supe'in
Morocco	モロッコ	morokko		Sri Lanka	スリランカ	suri ranka
Mozambique	モザンビーク	mozam-biiku		Sudan	スーダン	suudan
Myanmar	ミャンマー	myam'maa		Suriname	スリナム	suri-namu
Namibia	ナミビア	nami-bi'a		Swaziland	スワジランド	suwaji-rando
Nauru	ナウル	na'uru		Sweden	スウェーデン	suweeden
Nepal	ネパール	nepaaru		Switzerland	スイス	suisu
Netherlands	オランダ	oranda		Syria	シリア	shiri'a
New Zealand	ニュージーランド	nyuujii-rando		Taiwan	台湾	taiwan
Nicaragua	ニカラグア	nika-ragu'a		Tajikistan	タジキスタン	tajiki-sutan
Niger	ニジェール	nijeeru		Tanzania	タンザニア	tan-zani'a
Nigeria	ナイジェリア	nai-jeri'a		Thailand	タイ	tai
North Korea	北朝鮮	kita choosen		Timor-Leste	東ティモール	higashi timooru
Norway	ノルウェー	noruwee		Togo	トーゴ	toogo
Oman	オマーン	omaan		Tonga	トンガ	tonga
Pakistan	パキスタン	paki-sutan		Trinidad And Tobago	トリニダード・トバゴ	torini-daado tobago
Palau	パラオ	para'o		Tunisia	チュニジア	chu-niji'a
Panama	パナマ	panama		Turkey	トルコ	toruko
Papua New Guinea	パプアニューギニア	papu'a nyuu-gini'a		Turkmenistan	トルクメニスタン	toruku-meni-sutan
Paraguay	パラグアイ	para-gu'ai		Tuvalu	ツバル	tsubaru
Peru	ペルー	peruu		Uganda	ウガンダ	uganda
Philippines	フィリピン	firipin		Ukraine	ウクライナ	ukuraina
Poland	ポーランド	poo-rando		United Arab Emirates	アラブ首長国連邦	arabu shuchoo-koku rempoo

United Kingdom (Great Britain)	....英国..	eekoku		
	イギリス	igirisu		
United States .	アメリカ	amerika		
Uruguay ...	ウルグアイ	urugu'ai		
Uzbekistan ..	ウズベキスタン	uzubeki-sutan		
Vanuatu ...	バヌアツ	banuatsu		
Vatican City ..	バチカン市国 ...	bachikan shikoku		
Venezuela ..	ベネズエラ	bene-zuera		
Vietnam ...	ベトナム	betonamu		
Yemen	イエメン	i'emen		
Zambia....	ザンビア	zam-bi'a		
Zimbabwe ..	ジンバブウェ...	jim-babu'e		

2 Days of the Month (日にち / hi-nichi)

1st day of the month	1日	tsuitachi		16th	1 6日	juu-roku nichi
2nd	2日	futsuka		17th	1 7日	juu-shichi nichi
3rd	3日	mikka		18th	1 8日	juu-hachi nichi
4th	4日	yokka		19th	1 9日	juu-ku nichi
5th	5日	itsuka		20th	2 0日	hatsuka
6th	6日	muika		21th	2 1日	ni-juu-ichi nichi
7th	7日	nanoka		22th	2 2日	ni-juu-ni nichi
8th	8日	yooka		23th	2 3日	ni-juu-san nichi
9th	9日	kokonoka		24th	2 4日	ni-juu-yok-ka
10th	1 0日	tooka		25th	2 5日	ni-juu-go nichi
11th	1 1日	juu-ichi nichi		26th	2 6日	ni-juu-roku nichi
12th	1 2日	juu-ni nichi		27th	2 7日	ni-juu-shichi nichi
13th	1 3日	juu-san nichi		28th	2 8日	ni-juu-hachi nichi
14th	1 4日	juu-yokka		29th	2 9日	ni-juu-ku nichi
15th	1 5日	juu-go nichi		30th	3 0日	san-juu nichi
				31th	3 1日	san-juu-ichi nichi

3 Japanese Holidays (日本の休日 / nihon no kyuu-jitsu)

New Year's Day (Jan. 1)
..................元日 .... gan-jitsu
Coming of Age Day (2nd Mon. of Jan.)
...................成人の日 ..... seejin no hi
National Foundation Day (Feb. 11)
...................建国記念の日 kenkoku kinen no hi
Spring Equinox Day (around Mar. 21)
...................春分の日 ..... shumbun no hi
Showa Day (Apr. 29)
...................昭和の日 ..... showa no hi
Constitution Day (May 3)
...................憲法記念日 .. kempoo kinem-bi
Greenery Day (May 4)
...................みどりの日 .. midori no hi
Children's Day (May 5)
...................こどもの日 .. kodomo no hi

Marine Day (3rd Mon. of July)
...................海の日 .... umi no hi
Respect-for-the-Aged Day (3rd Mon. of Sep.)
...................敬老の日 ...... keeroo no hi
Autumnal Equinox Day (around Sep. 23)
...................秋分の日 . shuubun no hi
Health and Sports Day (2nd Mon. of Oct.)
...................体育の日 ..... tai'iku no hi
Culture Day (Nov. 3)
...................文化の日 ..... bunka no hi
Labor Thanksgiving Day (Nov. 23)
...................勤労感謝の日 kinroo kansha no hi
the Emperor's Birthday (Dec. 23)
...................天皇誕生日 .. ten'noo tanjoo-bi

4 Counting in Japanese (日本語の数の数え方 / nihon go no kazu no kazo'e-kata)

one hundred .	百（100）	hyaku		106	hyaku roku
	101	hyaku ichi		107	hyaku nana
	102	hyaku ni		108	hyaku hachi
	103	hyaku san		109	hyaku kyuu
	104	hyaku yon		110	hyaku juu
	105	hyaku go		111	hyaku juu-ichi

112	hyaku juu-ni
113	hyaku juu-san
114	hyaku juu-yon
115	hyaku juu-go
116	hyaku juu-roku
117	hyaku juu-nana
118	hyaku juu-hachi
119	hyaku juu-kyuu
120	hyaku ni-juu
200	ni-hyaku
300	san-byaku
400	yon-hyaku
500	go-hyaku
600	rop-pyaku
700	nana-hyaku
800	hap-pyaku
900	kyuu-hyaku
one thousand 千 (1,000)	sen
1,500	sen go-hyaku
2千 (2,000)	ni-sen
3千 (3,000)	san-zen
4千 (4,000)	yon-sen
5千 (5,000)	go-sen
6千 (6,000)	roku-sen
7千 (7,000)	nana-sen
8千 (8,000)	hassen
9千 (9,000)	kyuu-sen
ten thousand	
1万 (10,000)	ichi-man
1万5千 (15,000)	ichi-man go-sen
2万5千900 (25,900)	ni-man go-sen kyuu-hyaku
one hundred thousand	
10万 (100,000)	juu-man
20万 (200,000)	ni-juu-man
20万7千500 (207,500)	ni-jyuu-man nana-sen go-hyaku
one million	
100万 (1,000,000)	hyaku-man
ten million	
1千万 (10,000,000)	issen-man
one hundred million	
1億 (100,000,000)	ichi-oku
one billion	
10億 (1,000,000,000)	juu-oku
ten billion	
100億 (10,000,000,000)	hyaku-oku
one hundred billion	
1000億 (100,000,000,000)	sen-oku
one trillion	
1兆 (1,000,000,000,000)	icchoo

Acknowledgements and Author's Notes

I wish to express my most heartfelt gratitude to the following people.

Ms. Kae Murofushi, our talented artist and illustrator. She did all those fantastic illustrations for the phrasebook. She is one artist who knows how to "gambaru" for art's sake. I hope she likes the finished phrasebook as much as I do.

Mr. Robert Robison, my English-language resource person. Without his help I couldn't have translated all those tricky Japanese words and phrases. He is one "gaijin-san" who knows the virtue of "gaman" and hard work. His understanding of things Japanese is complimented by his Japanese wife, Kotomi-san, with whom he enjoys a Japanized lifestyle in a nice little "manshon" in downtown Tokyo.

Ms. Noriko Takamaru, my Japanese-language resource person. Her background as a Japanese language education major lends academic integrity to this phrasebook. She made meaningful suggestions on the Japanese words and phrases and did more than half of the "Romanizations" in the phrasebook.

I also want to thank YOU for reading my phrasebook. I had great fun making this phrasebook, and I hope you will have as much fun using it to talk to Japanese people you meet.

My editorial team and I wish you the best of luck with your Japanese study and intercultural communication.

Author
Toshiya Enomoto

協力者へのお礼と著者あとがき

　この本の制作に参加してくれた以下の皆さんに心からお礼を申し上げます。
　イラストの才能で貢献していただいた、むろふしかえさん。この本でフィーチャーされている素晴らしいイラストは、すべてむろふしさんの手によるものです。むろふしさんはまさにアートのために「ガンバル」人で、できあがった本を私と同じくらい気に入ってくれていることを願うばかりです。
　英語のリソースパーソンを務めてくれたロバート・ロビソンさん。翻訳しにくい日本語表現を英語に直す上で、彼の存在はきわめて重要でした。彼

はしっかりと仕事をしてくれる人で、「ガマン」という美徳も知っているガイジンさんです。ロブさんが日本的な事象に詳しいのは、ことみさんという日本人の奥さんのおかげで、2人は東京の下町にある小さな「マンション」に居を構えて、日本式の生活を楽しんでいます。

　日本語のリソースパーソンを務めてくれた高丸典子さん。日本語教育を専攻された高丸さんのおかげで、内容にアカデミックさが加わったように思います。収録した日本語について意味のある助言をしてくれただけではなく、"ローマ字化"も半分以上は高丸さんの功績です。

　この本を読んでくれた皆さんにも感謝します。とても楽しみながらつくることのできた本なので、皆さんも同じくらい楽しみながら日本人とのコミュニケーションに役立てていただければと思います。

　編集部のメンバーともども、みなさんの日本語学習と異文化コミュニケーションが素晴らしいものとなりますよう、お祈り申し上げます。

著者
榎本年弥

＊ You can contact Toshiya at enomomail@yahoo.co.jp
Be friendly and respectful and he'll be nice back to you.
＊著者にメールを出してみたい方は
enomomail@yahoo.co.jp までどうぞ。
なお、メールを送られる際には常識的なマナーをお守り下さい。

友達に"ニホンゴ"のプレゼントをしてみない？『旅の指さし会話帳 21 JAPAN』はオンラインで注文できます。弊社のホームページ https://www.yubisashi.com をご覧になるか、yubisashi@4jc.co.jp までお問い合わせのメールをどうぞ。

How about giving a gift of "nihon-go" to your friends? You can order "The Original POINT-AND-SPEAK Phrasebook 21 JAPAN"online.Visit us at http://www.yubisashi.com or drop us an email at yubisashi@4jc.co.jp

Author 著者◎ Toshiya Enomoto 榎本年弥

Author Toshiya Enomoto calls himself an "on-the-street" linguist and a 100% genuine native-born Japanese Japan observer. His keen awareness of things Japanese and rather un-Japanese sense of humor has won him a place in many an international reader's heart. Toshiya has also written "The Original Point-and-Speak Phrasebook 7 Australia,","The Original Point-and-Speak Phrasebook 9 U.S.A.", "The Original Point-and-Speak Phrasebook of Love English Edition" for Yubisashi Co., Ltd.

自称"ストリート系"語学スペシャリスト。100％本物の日本生まれの日本ウォッチャーである。日本的な事象に対する鋭い観察眼と、日本人らしからぬユーモアのセンスで、多くの海外の読者に支持されている。主な著書に、「旅の指さし会話帳⑦オーストラリア」、「旅の指さし会話帳⑩アメリカ」、「恋する指さし会話帳①英語編」（共に小社刊）などがある。

Illustrations by Kae Murofushi, Junko Nagata
Photography by Toshiya Enomoto
Book Desgin by Michiaki Saeki
Map Design by WORDSOUT
Resource Persons: Robert Robison and Noriko Takamaru

The author would also like to say "arigatoo" to Yuichiro & Joan Hoashi, Kotomi "Tsukaya" Robison, Naoki Fudoji, Frank Burjan, John Cassells, Andrew J. Nichols, Yoko Nomura (Usagi-sha), Tommy Usukura, and Yayoi & Toshiharu Enomoto.

イラスト	むろふしかえ	
	http://murofushi-kae.com	
	永田純子	
写真	榎本年弥	
ブックデザイン	佐伯通昭	
	http://www.knickknack.jp	
地図作成	ワーズアウト	
リソースパーソン	ロバート・ロビソン	
	高丸典子	
Special thanks to:	帆足勇一郎＆ジョアン	
	ことみ"塚谷"ロビソン	
	不動寺直樹	
	フランク・バージョン	
	ジョン・カッセルズ	
	アンドリューJニコルズ	
	野村陽子（ウサギ舎）	
	呉玲華	
	トミー臼倉	
	榎本年春＆弥生	

ここ以外のどこかへ！
旅の指さし会話帳21JAPAN

2001年　9月　10日　第1刷
2024年　6月　2日　第59刷

著者 ───────
榎本年弥

発行者 ───────
田村隆宗

発行所 ───────
株式会社ゆびさし
〒151-0053 東京都渋谷区代々木1-30-15
天翔代々木ビル S607
電話 03-6324-1234
振替 00140-4-46236　https://www.yubisashi.com

印刷 ───────
モリモト印刷株式会社

ⓒ 2001 Toshiya Enomoto
ISBN978-4-7958-1843-9
落丁本・乱丁本はお取替えいたします。

※「旅の指さし会話帳」及び「YUBISASHI」は、
（株）ゆびさしの登録商標です。
※「YUBISASHI」は国際商標登録済みです。